RICHARD M.
NIXON

OTHER BOOKS IN THE PRESIDENTS AND THEIR DECISIONS SERIES

William J. Clinton
Lyndon B. Johnson
Ronald Reagan
Franklin D. Roosevelt

RICHARD M. NIXON

JEFF HAY, *Book Editor*

DAVID L. BENDER, *Publisher*
BRUNO LEONE, *Executive Editor*
BONNIE SZUMSKI, *Editorial Director*
STUART B. MILLER, *Managing Editor*
JAMES D. TORR, *Series Editor*

❧

GREENHAVEN PRESS, INC.
SAN DIEGO, CALIFORNIA

Every effort has been made to trace the owners of copyrighted material. The articles in this volume may have been edited for content, length, and/or reading level. The titles have been changed to enhance the editorial purpose.

No part of this book may be reproduced or used in any form or by any means, electrical, mechanical, or otherwise, including, but not limited to, photocopy, recording, or any information on storage and retrieval system without prior written permission from the publisher.

Library of Congress Cataloging-in-Publication Data

Richard Nixon / Jeff Hay, book editor.
    p.   cm. — (Presidents and their decisions)
    Includes bibliographical references and index.
    ISBN 0-7377-0405-5 (lib. : alk. paper) — ISBN 0-7377-0404-7 (pbk. : alk. paper)
    1. Nixon, Richard M. (Richard Milhous), 1913–1994. 2. United States—Politics and government—1969–1974—Decision making. I. Hay, Jeff. II. Series.

E855 .R53 2001
973.924'092—dc21   00-022324
                                                  CIP

Series Design: LiMiTeD Edition Book Design, Linda Mae Tratechaud

©2001 Greenhaven Press, Inc.
P.O. Box 289009, San Diego, CA 92198-9009

PRINTED IN THE U.S.A.

Contents

Foreword   9

Richard M. Nixon: A Biography   12

Chapter 1: Nixon and the Environmental Movement

1. Nixon: A Reluctant Environmentalist
   by Charles S. Warren   45

   Though not an environmentalist, Nixon responded to the
   widespread environmental movement with the creation
   of such institutions as the Environmental Protection
   Agency.

2. The Nixon Administration Responded Quickly to
   Environmental Concerns *by John C. Whitaker*   54

   Nixon attacked environmental problems head-on by creating a task force to develop his environmental strategy.
   The task force pinpointed such problems as air and water
   pollution, an d recommended the creation of the Environmental Protection Agency.

3. Congress Rather than Nixon Should Be Credited
   for Environmental Action *by Jerry Voorhis*   63

   Nixon always tried to balance environmental policies
   against the needs of business and industry, but he usually
   favored the latter. Most of the credit for environmental
   reforms should go to Congress.

4. Nixon's Environmental Policies Reflected the
   Will of the American People *by Tom Wicker*   69

   As president, Nixon was a pragmatist who felt he was
   required to respond to the wishes of the American
   people on environmental issues.

Chapter 2: Trying to End the Vietnam War

1. Nixon Secretly Expanded U.S. Involvement in
   Vietnam *by Joan Hoff*   79

   Instead of ending the Vietnam War as he had promised
   during his 1968 election campaign, Nixon escalated it
   with the secret and illegal bombing of Cambodia in 1969.

2. Nixon Planned to End the War Through
   Vietnamization
   by Norman Podhoretz   93

   In order to reduce U.S. involvement in Vietnam, Nixon
   wanted America's South Vietnamese allies to take over
   responsibility for the war. This policy, known as Vietnamization, required the slow withdrawal of American
   forces combined with the training and arming of South
   Vietnamese troops.

3. The Antiwar Movement Forced Nixon to Pull
   Back in Vietnam *by Charles DeBenedetti
   and Charles Chatfield*   99

   The already vocal and active antiwar movement staged its
   most widespread protests after Nixon gave support to the
   South Vietnamese invasion of Cambodia in 1970. In
   response to this outcry, Nixon restricted his support of
   the invasion and committed to an even faster withdrawal
   of American troops.

4. Nixon Dealt with the Antiwar Movement
   Effectively *by Adam Garfinkle*   107

   Nixon responded to students' antiwar protests by ending
   the draft and reaffirming his commitment to withdraw
   American troops.

5. Nixon's Tragic Insistence on Peace with Honor
   by Michael A. Genovese   114

   Although Nixon wanted to end the war in Vietnam, he
   believed that to concede defeat in the conflict would
   encourage aggression in other parts of the world. In a
   tragic reversal, the peace settlement the Nixon adminis-

tration agreed to left South Vietnam at the mercy of
the North.

CHAPTER 3: NIXON'S VISIT TO CHINA

1. Nixon's Opening of China Was a Major
   Accomplishment *by Cecil V. Crabb Jr.* 124
   Nixon's re-establishment of normal diplomatic relations
   with the People's Republic of China was a major
   improvement in international relations.

2. Both China and America Gained by Nixon's
   Attempts to Establish Normal Relations
   by Robert G. Sutter 129
   Both China and America gained from the good relations
   between Nixon and Chinese Communist leaders Mao
   Tse-Tung and Chou En-Lai. China acquired a leadership
   role in East Asia while America was able to reduce Cold
   War hostilities and improve its strategic position in Asia.

3. Nixon's Withdrawal from Vietnam Made His
   Opening of China Possible *by Joseph Camilleri* 136
   Nixon succeeded in improving U.S.-Chinese relations only
   after he had moved away from the U.S. policy of "containing" communism to nations where it already existed.

4. Nixon's Policy Toward China Was Self-Serving
   by George W. Ball 145
   Rather than the result of great foresight, Nixon's opening
   of China was a public relations ploy that took advantage
   of good timing.

CHAPTER 4: THE WATERGATE SCANDAL AND THE END OF NIXON'S PRESIDENCY

1. Nixon Used the Presidency to Exercise Personal
   Power *by Arthur G. Neal* 154
   As president, Nixon wanted to act without interference
   from Congress or the federal bureaucracy. This attitude

forts, from 1972 to 1974, to cover up the involvement of his aides in the Watergate scandal.

Most of the truly history-making presidential decisions, though, remain the subject of intense scrutiny and historical debate. Many of these were made during a time of war or other crisis, in which a president was forced to risk either spectacular success or devastating failure. Examples include Lincoln's much-scrutinized handling of the crisis at Fort Sumter, the first conflict of the Civil War; FDR's efforts to aid the European Allies at the beginning of World War II; Harry Truman's controversial decision to use the atomic bomb in order to end that conflict; and Lyndon Johnson's fateful decision to escalate the war in Vietnam.

Each volume in the Presidents and Their Decisions series devotes a full chapter to each of the president's key decisions. The essays in each chapter, most written by presidential historians and biographers, offer a range of perspectives on the president and his actions. Some provide background on the political, social, and economic factors behind a particular decision. Others critique the president's performance, offering a negative or positive appraisal. Essays have been chosen for their concise and engaging presentation of the facts, and each is preceded by a straightforward summary of the article's content.

In addition to the articles, these books include extensive material to help the student researcher. An opening essay provides both a brief biography of the president and an overview of the events that occurred during his time in office. A chronology also helps readers keep track of the dates of specific events. A comprehensive index and an annotated table of contents aid readers in quickly locating material of interest, and an extensive bibliography serves as a launching point for further research. Finally, an appendix of primary historical documents provides a sampling of the president's most important speeches, as well as some of his contemporaries' criticisms.

Greenhaven Press's Presidents and Their Decisions series will help students gain a deeper understanding of the decisions made by some of the most influential leaders in American history.

RICHARD M. NIXON: A BIOGRAPHY

SHORTLY AFTER NOON ON AUGUST 9, 1974, RICHARD M. Nixon, the former president of the United States, stepped aboard the presidential helicopter *Marine One*. He turned around to give a last wave and smile to the American public and the television cameras. Then he flew off into exile. Nixon's presidency had ended earlier that day in his resignation from office as a result of the Watergate scandal.

The American presidency is inherently controversial, yet Nixon, president from January 1969 until August 1974, had an exceptional ability to attract controversy as well as create enemies. To many, Nixon seemed to be a shameless, amoral manipulator in search of greater and greater personal power. To others, however, Nixon was a great statesman. He was, they claimed, a foreign policy expert, as well as a pragmatist who believed in serving the American people, as he was elected to do, in the face of constant opposition, criticism, and mind-boggling red tape. Nixon's presidential legacy is indeed complex.

Nixon's Early Life

Richard Milhous Nixon was born on January 9, 1913. At that time his family lived in Yorba Linda, California, although they soon moved to nearby Whittier. Frank, Nixon's father, was largely unsuccessful in his work life; sometimes he was a grocer, sometimes a day laborer. He was, nonetheless, a strong-willed and stubborn parent. His mother Hannah was an extremely devout Quaker, and she brought up the family within that faith. Richard, named after King Richard the Lionheart of England, was the second of five sons.

The young Nixon was a very successful student, finishing third in his high school class. He had hoped to go on to college at Yale, but even though there was talk of scholarships to help pay tuition, Nixon and his family decided that the costs of travel and living would be too high. He attended Whittier College instead, a local institution affiliated with Quakerism.

Nixon's outstanding academic performance continued at Whittier, where he finished second in his graduating class with a major in constitutional history. The future president completed his education at Duke University Law School in North Carolina, where he specialized in constitutional law. In his second year at law school, Nixon was named president of the Duke Bar Association.

Upon the completion of his education, Nixon failed to find a job in New York City as he had hoped. He therefore returned to southern California and joined a Whittier law firm. In 1938, during participation in a local amateur dramatic society, Nixon met Pat Ryan. She was a vivacious young woman then teaching at Whittier High School. The two were married in June of 1940. Richard and Pat Nixon had two daughters, Julie and Patricia.

The Beginning of Nixon's Political Career

After serving as a naval officer in the Pacific during World War II, Nixon returned to Whittier. There he was approached by local Republican party leaders. They asked if he might be interested in running for the House of Representatives in 1946. Nixon assented and was elected over the Democratic candidate Jerry Voorhis. This was the first step in a rapid rise to success in national politics.

Nixon first gained fame on a national level with his involvement in the Alger Hiss case in the late 1940s. The period was one of intense anti-communism in the United States, and Nixon himself was beginning to think that communism was a threat to freedom and world peace. Alger Hiss was a highly respected former adviser to President Franklin D. Roosevelt. He had been accused of being a Communist by one Whitaker Chambers, an editor at Time Life, who had Communist ties himself.

In 1948, Hiss was summoned to testify before the House Committee on Un-American Activities, of which Nixon was a member. He claimed that not only was he not a Communist, he had never even heard of Whitaker Chambers. Although Hiss's denials cast a bad light on the committee, Nixon chose to soldier on: Through continued investigations into the backgrounds of both Hiss and Chambers, Nixon was ultimately able to establish that Hiss had lied before the committee, and Hiss was ultimately imprisoned for perjury.

Thanks to his actions in the case, Nixon acquired a great deal of national attention. Just as importantly, he proved himself as both a committed anti-Communist and a politician willing to take on difficult battles. Nixon's combative nature was already apparent; it was to be a major feature of his public life.

Nixon was quick to build on his newfound notoriety. When a *Los Angeles Times* writer suggested he run for the Senate in 1950, he jumped at the chance. Again, Nixon won. Only two years later, in 1952, Nixon found himself being considered as a possible running mate to Republican presidential hopeful Dwight D. Eisenhower. Eisenhower's staffers and other Republican leaders were quick to notice the assets Nixon had displayed in the Hiss case, his anti-communism and political tenacity. He was duly chosen as Eisenhower's vice-presidential running mate.

The Checkers Speech

The young and ambitious Nixon faced his first major political and personal crisis in the 1952 presidential campaign. It culminated in a public address known as the Checkers speech.

During the campaign, members of the press accused

Nixon of profiting personally from a fund of $22,000 set up by a group of one hundred California businessmen. Although an independent investigation later found Nixon innocent of any wrongdoing, many in the press, including writers at the influential *Washington Post*, asked Nixon to resign from the Republican ticket. Instead, he made a nationally televised speech in which he defended himself. He insisted that he had not benefited financially from any political activities. In sentimental tones, he explained that instead of a mink coat, for instance, his wife Pat owned merely "a respectable Republican cloth coat." Nixon went on to point out that one political gift he had received was from a supporter in Texas. It was a small cocker spaniel that six-year-old Tricia had named Checkers. Nixon proclaimed that he was not a quitter, but that he would resign from the ticket if necessary for the good of the Republican party.

The effect of the Checkers speech was extraordinary. The address was watched by an audience of 58 million, the largest television audience ever to that date. And support for Nixon was overwhelming. He had demonstrated that he was a devoted family man and an example of the national success a boy from a poor family could have in the United States. Nixon stayed on the Republican ticket, which went on to victory in the 1952 presidential election and won again in 1956.

In only six years Richard Milhous Nixon had risen from being a member of a Whittier, California, law firm to being vice president of the United States. He was at the leading edge of a younger generation of Republican leaders, he had proven himself a strong anti-Communist who knew that America had to be actively involved in world affairs, and he had learned that modern politics involves intense combat. Nixon's future appeared bright.

As vice president, Nixon continued to develop as a top-level statesman and politician. He was involved in a steady stream of domestic and international crises ranging from the Army-McCarthy hearings of 1954 to the Suez Crisis of 1956 to a near assault by a hostile crowd in Caracas, Venezuela, in 1958. On two occasions, Nixon found himself on the brink of the presidency itself: In 1954, Eisenhower had a heart attack and in 1957, a stroke. Many have considered Nixon, in fact, to be one of the most active vice presidents ever, taking part in cabinet discussions and meeting with high-level foreign dignitaries such as Soviet premier Nikita Krushchev. As the 1960 presidential election approached, and along with it Eisenhower's departure from the White House, it became clear that Nixon would be the Republican candidate.

Election Losses and a Retreat from Politics

The 1960 presidential election was one of the closest in American history. Nixon faced an opponent, John F. Kennedy, who was also young and energetic, and who, like Nixon, had mastered the use of television as a political weapon. In televised debates, Nixon came off badly against his opponent, partly because Nixon appeared sullen and unshaven. In November, Nixon lost the election by only 113,000 votes.

In 1961, Nixon and his family returned to California. There, he briefly practiced law before being bitten again by the political bug. He decided to run for governor of California in 1962. Again, he lost. Perhaps frustrated by the events of the last years, Nixon declared at a post-election press conference that reporters "would not have Nixon to kick around anymore." Many people seemed to think that Nixon's political career was finished. He moved his family back across the country to New York City, where he engaged in business and law.

Some have called the period from 1963 to 1967 the "wilderness years" for Nixon, implying that he was left out in the political cold. But in fact Nixon continued his political education, particularly in the field of international policy. During the period he had numerous meetings with world leaders, took several trips overseas, and wrote articles and made speeches on foreign affairs. He paid particular attention to the growing conflict in Vietnam. Also, in New York, he was in a position to expand his political base by building fund-raising networks and establishing other important contacts. After a successful Republican showing in the mid-term election of 1966, Nixon felt ready to run for president again.

The nation, however, had changed. The United States underwent a major transformation in the period between Nixon's gubernatorial loss in California and his decision to run for president in 1968. What had seemed to be a stable nation in danger only from the outside now seemed to be falling apart from within. John F. Kennedy had been assassinated in 1963, and his successor, Lyndon B. Johnson, won a landslide victory in 1964. Johnson tried to put in place the Great Society program, with which he hoped to liberalize American society and government. In addition, Johnson expanded American involvement in the conflict between the North Vietnamese Communists and their enemies in South Vietnam.

Back home, a young generation, that of the post–World War II "baby boomers," was coming of age. They were open to a more liberated lifestyle than Nixon's contemporaries had experienced, and were used to economic prosperity. Many of the young did not hesitate to protest injustices, whether domestic or international. A major focus of their protests was the war in Vietnam, where by 1968 many of their peers were serving and dying. Aside from the Vietnam War, young people were concerned about such issues as minority rights, greater equality for women, and environmental pollution.

When Nixon made the decision to run for president in 1968, the national atmosphere was therefore quite different than it had been in 1960. Yet Nixon felt he was up to the challenge; indeed, the new atmosphere perhaps appealed to his combative instincts. After a series of easy primary victories, he won the Republican nomination rather easily.

Nixon also managed to remain aloof from the various crises of 1968, which included the assassinations of Dr. Martin Luther King Jr. and Robert Kennedy, John F. Kennedy's brother, who was the front-runner for the Democratic nomination. Nixon, indeed, was able to stand by, and perhaps benefit from, various problems on the Democratic side. Shamed by his failure to reduce the conflict in Vietnam, Lyndon Johnson chose not to run again. And in the summer of 1968, the Democratic National Convention in Chicago was the site of violent protests. The Democrats finally settled on Hubert H. Humphrey, a senator from Minnesota, as Nixon's opponent.

Nixon ran a successful campaign with the help of his longtime aide, H.R. Haldeman. The race was close, but in the end Nixon was victorious. After the many triumphs and frustrations of the last 22 years, Nixon had finally been elected to the highest office in the land.

Nixon as President

Nixon's approach to the presidency was essentially pragmatic rather than ideological. In order to address problems and enforce laws that were already on the books, Nixon wanted a strong presidency. He did not want to be limited by Congress, by the extensive federal bureaucracy and its endless red tape, and by political niceties. Consequently, Nixon relied mostly on advisers and friends rather than on congressional leaders or government bureaucrats. He placed loyal supporters in key positions, such as chief of staff or cabinet secretary, and tended to find work for people he respected. Many Nixon supporters, such as Maurice Stans, found themselves in a variety of positions during the administration.

Nixon relied mostly, however, on a very close circle of

staffers. Most important among them were H.R. Haldeman, Nixon's chief of staff, and John Ehrlichman, his main domestic policy adviser. In foreign policy, Nixon avoided the State Department in favor of his national security adviser Henry Kissinger. Other members of Nixon's inner circle included Melvin Laird, the secretary of defense, and attorney general John Mitchell, a longtime friend.

Nixon's reliance on close loyalists was partly due to his wish to streamline governmental procedures and avoid as much red tape as possible. He remembered, as vice president, sitting in on innumerable unwieldy and unproductive cabinet meetings. In addition, he was a relative outsider in Washington, D.C., facing a hostile Congress. He believed that by creating a strong executive branch, and making it possible for cabinet secretaries and other officials to do their jobs with minimal interference, he could be a more effective president. He even went so far as to initiate a "new federalism," in which important government programs would be shifted from Washington, D.C., to the individual states.

This approach has garnered Nixon a great deal of criticism. Some have claimed he tried to create a sort of presidential dictatorship. Others have accused him of seeing the presidency as a place where he could exercise personal and willful authority without the traditional checks and balances of American politics. To some, Nixon seemed to be showing blatant disrespect for Congress and for the federal government in general. Moreover, in trying to carry out his more streamlined approach to the government, Nixon sometimes not only stepped on people's toes, he crossed the line into illegal acts.

In addition, Nixon's approach helped to inspire an us-against-them mentality among White House staffers and advisers. Loyalty to Nixon personally, rather than experience or competence, became the main avenue to success within the administration. Beyond that, Nixon provided an example to his staffers; they saw his competitiveness and how he was willing to use questionable or devious tactics. Indeed, some of Nixon's men following the president's example and, believing they were acting in his best interests, initiated the scandal that ended his presidency.

Domestic Policies

Among the areas where Nixon's pragmatic approach to the presidency is clear is domestic policy. Unlike other Republican leaders, Nixon was a "liberal" in certain areas of domestic policy. He believed that if the American people were concerned about an issue, it was his job to address it, ideology or party necessity aside. Nixon was active in, among other areas, environmental policy and civil rights.

The environment had only emerged as a political and social issue during the 1960s. Books like Rachel Carson's *Silent Spring* had pointed out the dangers of chemical pollutants, and growing numbers of Americans were concerned about smoggy cities and dangerous drinking water. Environmental activists had gone so far by Nixon's administration, in fact, as to create a holiday to increase awareness of environmental issues; the first Earth Day was held in April 1970.

Although Nixon was not particularly aware of the environment, his domestic policy adviser, John Ehrlichman, was. Ehrlichman had been a land-use lawyer in Seattle, and he brought the issue to the president's attention. Nixon, knowing that the American people were concerned, began to act according to his strategy of using presidential power and influence rather than the federal bureaucracy or Congress. Instead of seeking legislation, he formed a group of advisers to set up environmental policy guidelines.

In his State of the Union address in January 1970, Nixon included a powerful environmental message. He claimed that a clean environment was "the birthright of every American" and proposed a huge funding increase to help clean up water as well as new restrictions on air pollution. *Time* magazine, in the following months, even referred to Nixon as an environmental president.

While Nixon was sympathetic to the desires of the American people for environmental action, his pragmatism required him to balance environmental measures against their impact on the economy. Nixon was a strongly pro-business president, and generally opposed federal regulation of the private sector. He believed, fundamentally, that jobs were more important than the environment. Thus he hesitated to apply restrictions on business, such as air pollution controls on the automobile industry. In addition, he insisted that environmental measures be subject to cost-benefit analyses conducted by the Office of Management and Budget, an institution he created in hopes of reigning in the federal bureaucracy. This strategy garnered him criticism from strong environmentalists.

Nonetheless, Nixon responded to the public call for action in ways that suited him: He established governmental agencies, encouraged environmental studies and clean-up actions in federal facilities, and where appropriate, supported federal legislation, such as the Clean Air Act of 1970. Also, he relied on his close advisers rather than other politicians or environmental experts.

A Civil Rights President

Nixon was also a strong advocate of civil rights. In addition to being the first president to enforce affirmative action in federal hiring and contracting, Nixon did a great deal to integrate the public schools, helping finish business begun in 1954 with the Supreme Court's *Brown v. Board of Education* decision, which declared that racially separate but equal education was unconstitutional. One of the measures the Supreme Court had authorized to integrate schools was busing, in which African-American students from poorer school districts might be taken by bus to wealthier white districts. Conversely, white students could be bused to mostly African-American areas.

Nixon knew that many Americans, including southern Democratic voters he hoped to attract, disliked busing. At the same time, he wanted to enforce the *Brown* decision, and he believed that integration was necessary to help contain racial conflict. In order to solve the problem, Nixon focused the issue on educational quality rather than race, and he urged states to find ways to integrate schools without busing. To encourage this, he often withheld or doled out federal funds. Among his recommendations was that the borders of school districts be withdrawn to include both African-American and white students in more equal proportions. While the Supreme Court still maintained that busing was a good way to integrate the schools, Nixon urged that busing only be used as a last resort; he even tried to pass legislation against it.

Despite the ongoing controversy over busing, however, school integration remains one of the Nixon administration's great domestic achievements. By 1972 most public schools were integrated, whereas in 1968, before Nixon was elected, 68 percent of African-American children in the South attended separate schools.

Finally, by executive order in 1969, Nixon established the Office of Minority Business Enterprise (OMBE). He hoped to use the OMBE to help members of minority groups start and maintain their own businesses. It was first directed by a Nixon loyalist, Maurice Stans, who was first secretary of commerce but later Nixon's 1972 campaign finance director. Although the OMBE had many critics, and perhaps raised unrealistic expectations, within a few years it had helped established over fifty minority business investment companies where entrepreneurs could seek low-interest loans. The bulk of the funding for the investment companies came not from the federal treasury but from corporations. Long after Nixon's resignation, at a meeting in the 1980s, hundreds of African-American and Latino businessmen and women gratefully acknowledged the help of the OMBE.

Nixon's civil rights activities were clearly consistent, again, with his overall approach to the presidency. As a pragmatist, he was more interested in real-world results than in ideology, and in using presidential power to enforce laws that were already on the books, like school integration and affirmative action. He also clung to the American tradition of self-help. For a leader like Nixon, a measure like the OMBE was more attractive than dealing with more radical civil rights activists such as the Black Panthers, even though that might have attracted more media attention. In addition, it was natural for Nixon to seek to help minority businesses by executive order and through a trusted insider such as Stans.

Nixon's Foreign Policy

Foreign rather than domestic policy was, however, Nixon's greater political fascination. The interest dated back to Nixon's days in the House of Representatives and had survived the many ups and downs in his political career. In or out of office, Nixon had traveled overseas, maintained contact with foreign leaders, and kept informed on foreign policy issues. Many historians would later argue that aside from the Watergate scandal, foreign policy is where Nixon left his greatest mark as president. Among the major legacies of his administration was détente with the Soviet Union, the establishment of open diplomatic relations with the People's Republic of China, and, for good or ill, the extrication of the United States from the Vietnam War.

Nixon's foreign policy was built on the principle of "linkage" between the five regions of the world which had the greatest economic power and the greatest stake in world peace: the United States, Western Europe, the Soviet

Union, Japan, and China. His overall goal was to make it possible for those areas to negotiate and do business with one another. He hoped that such an arrangement would discourage conflicts like the Vietnam War, increase prosperity, and tone down Cold War hostilities.

Indeed, Nixon's political career had coincided with the first three decades of the Cold War and in many ways was shaped by the struggle. The Cold War not only trained Nixon to be strongly anti-Communist, it taught him that the United States had to be willing to project power in the world in order to defend freedom. As president, Nixon combined this background with his consistent pragmatism. He wanted to continue to oppose communism, but he also realized that the United States had to live with two Communist superpowers: the Soviet Union and the People's Republic of China.

Nixon Was a Product of the Cold War

The Cold War had its roots in World War II. While the young Nixon was stationed in the Pacific, the Soviet Union, after pushing Hitler's Nazis out of Eastern Europe, remained there and sponsored the emergence of local Communist regimes. Nations from Poland to Bulgaria soon became Communist allies of the Soviets. The United States and its allies in Western Europe grew afraid that communism was a threat to free countries everywhere. Nixon was able to observe this firsthand, when as a young congressman he visited Europe as part of a congressional committee investigating aid to European countries.

In this context, American leaders developed the policy of containment, under which Western nations tried to restrict communism to the nations which already practiced it, and to oppose, with force when necessary, the spread of communism to new countries. The policy of containment, among other things, contributed to American involvement in the Korean War in the early 1950s and the Vietnam War in the 1960s.

The containment policy received a severe blow in 1949 when Mao Tse-tung's Communist forces in China defeated Chiang Kai-shek's Nationalists, who were supported by the United States. Mao inaugurated the People's Republic of China while the Nationalists were forced into exile on the island of Taiwan. The young Nixon was only one of many who accused American liberals of "losing" China to Mao and the Communists. In the meantime, the United States refused to recognize the People's Republic and helped give China's place in the United Nations to the Nationalists in Taiwan.

A second blow to containment also came in 1949 when the Soviet Union announced that it had successfully tested an atomic bomb. No longer did the United States have a monopoly on nuclear power. For the next forty years the United States and the Soviet Union engaged in an arms race, seeking to build not only more and stronger nuclear bombs but also better ways of delivering them to potential enemies.

In the early 1950s, the Soviet Union and the People's Republic of China were friends and allies, and communism seemed to be spreading. Nixon, after a 1953 trip to Asia, came to believe that the United States had to step into the void then being created by the retreating European colonial empires, which had controlled Asia since the 1800s. Otherwise, he argued, smaller nations like Vietnam would be taken over by local Communist insurgents who were supported by the two Communist giants. Asia, in the language of the day, would become a continent of falling dominoes, with one nation after another falling into Communist hands. Nixon supported the majority view that the United States had to step in to prevent that.

The Long War in Vietnam

The test case for the domino theory, and Nixon's greatest foreign policy challenge, was Vietnam. After World War II,

Vietnam remained a French colony, part of French Indochina. However, an independence group in the northern part of the country, led by Ho Chi Minh, soon engaged the French in an anti-colonial war. Ho Chi Minh was a Communist, though not a very enthusiastic one, and he soon received support from the Soviets and from Mao. The anti-colonial conflict soon turned into a civil war, with Ho's northern Vietnamese arrayed against a French puppet regime based in Saigon in southern Vietnam.

Ho's forces won a decisive victory against the French at Dien Bien Phu in 1954, and the French were forced out of the country. The subsequent peace agreement divided Vietnam, however, into two separate countries, pending further agreements and elections. Ho's Communist Democratic Republic of Vietnam, generally known as North Vietnam, dominated the north of the country. In the south, a regime allied with the United States took hold. South Vietnam was strongly anti-Communist, but for most of its short history it was a corrupt and unstable dictatorship.

From the beginning the United States supported the government of South Vietnam in accordance with the demands of the containment policy. President John F. Kennedy, a staunch cold warrior, decided in the early 1960s that more support was necessary. By then, the civil war in Vietnam had sprung up again with the emergence of the Vietcong, supporters of Ho Chi Minh who lived in the south. By 1963, Kennedy had sent 15,000 military advisers to assist the South Vietnamese in opposing both North Vietnam and the Vietcong.

Kennedy's successor, Lyndon B. Johnson, decided to escalate the American commitment to South Vietnam. Between 1965 and 1968, Johnson authorized hundreds of bombing raids on North Vietnamese and Vietcong positions. There were also occasional secret bombings of neighboring Cambodia and Laos. In addition to the bombings, Johnson sent to Vietnam huge numbers of

American troops. By 1968, there were a half million American troops in the area, some of whom began to fall victim to the conflict. Johnson's show of force failed when, at the time of "Tet," the Vietnamese new year, in January 1968, the North Vietnamese launched a huge and reasonably successful offensive against the south. The resulting casualties further enflamed an already strong antiwar movement in the United States. Johnson, in response, chose not to run for re-election.

During the mid-1960s Nixon was out of office, but he had kept himself informed on the Vietnam situation. He made visits to the South Vietnamese capital of Saigon in 1964 and 1965. There, he expressed surprise at the ineptitude and inefficiency of the war efforts of both the South Vietnamese and their American supporters. He pledged during his election campaign in 1968 to end the war quickly.

Better Relations with the Soviet Union

Once Nixon was inaugurated in January of 1969, he began to implement his policy of linkage. First, he wanted to create an environment in which the United States and the Soviet Union could negotiate reasonably and productively. Along with national security adviser Henry Kissinger, Nixon realized that the nuclear arms race with the Soviets had reached a sort of plateau; both countries had the ability to destroy not only each other but much of the world with nuclear weapons. Consequently, it was in the interests not only of superpower relations but world peace that the United States and the Soviet Union communicate with one another reasonably. With the possibility of nuclear destruction, an intolerant stance on communism was no longer practical.

Nixon and Kissinger began to pursue a policy known as détente, a French term for "a relaxing of tensions." Détente was short on specific goals and long-term effects, yet it did result in certain shifts in American-Soviet relations.

There were three summit meetings, for instance, between President Nixon and Soviet Premier Leonid Brezhnev. The two developed, in fact, a friendly personal relationship. In addition, détente helped to bring about the first formal discussions on ending the arms race with the so-called Strategic Arms Limitation Treaty, or SALT I, talks. There were even, thanks to Nixon's policies, greater trade opportunities between the two superpowers. As ever, Nixon's approach was pragmatic; although détente accomplished little in terms of specifics (even SALT I was shot down in Congress), it helped to open up relations between the United States and the Soviet Union, and may have helped reduce the risk of conflict involving the two.

Nixon was also pragmatic in his approach to China, although in this instance he opened himself up to charges of hypocrisy. As congressman and vice president Nixon was a vocal critic of Communist China, and supported the United States in isolating China diplomatically. Yet as president Nixon went out of his way to end that isolation. He realized that circumstances had changed by the late 1960s. First, China and the Soviet Union were no longer friendly; they no longer made up a dominant and threatening Communist bloc. Second, with the quagmire in Vietnam, the United States had begun to abandon the containment policy. Finally, China itself was ready to open up to the world.

Beginning in 1965, China underwent a so-called Cultural Revolution. This was an attempt by the aging Mao Tse-tung to re-invigorate revolutionary ideology and re-energize the nation by focusing on the young. Groups of young "red guards" rampaged through the streets destroying cultural artifacts, attacking "counter-revolutionaries," and often even harassing their own parents and teachers. Revolutionary Committees replaced more traditional government agencies. The Cultural Revolution, however, largely failed to improve China's economy or administration. Moreover, it seemed to demonstrate the limits of radical revolutionary ideology. Many in the West viewed the excesses of the Cultural Revolution as proof of the evils of "Red China" and the need to support the aging Nationalists in Taiwan. But Nixon felt the time was ripe to reconsider America's stance toward Mao and the People's Republic. As president, Nixon claimed that the Chinese were a great and powerful people who could no longer be isolated from the world. He argued in a 1970 foreign policy report to Congress that improving American relations with China would improve chances for peace not only in Asia but worldwide. Nixon hoped, he said, to make a visit to China personally. The Chinese themselves, through intermediaries, made it known that they would be open to such a visit, particularly after Nixon showed his good faith by withdrawing American troops from Vietnam.

Ping-Pong Diplomacy

In April 1971 Americans began hearing about "ping-pong" diplomacy in the newspapers and on television. A break in U.S.-Chinese relations was reached when an American table tennis team, visiting Japan for the world championships, was invited to compete in China. Nixon, however, wanted to keep his own ping-pong diplomacy secret. Kissinger was dispatched on a secret mission to the Chinese capital of Peking to arrange a meeting between Nixon and the Chinese leaders, Chairman Mao of the Chinese Communist Party and Premier Chou En-lai. Nixon arrived in Peking in February 1972.

Nixon's visit to China was a huge public relations victory, garnering approval from most Americans. The president not only established a good personal relationship with Mao and Chou, who admired Nixon as a statesman, he restored normal diplomatic relations as well as trade opportunities between the United States and China. Nixon has been criticized for keeping his overtures to China secret from American allies (particularly Japan) and for selling out the Taiwanese Nationalists, but his role in ending China's diplomatic isolation remains perhaps the greatest single accomplishment of his presidency.

Seeking Peace with Honor in Vietnam

The extrication of the United States from the Vietnam War proved, however, to be a larger problem. Indeed, when he was elected Nixon inherited a huge problem in Vietnam. An American force of half a million was in Vietnam trying to prop up a collapsing South Vietnamese dictatorship. In addition, American involvement in the conflict had inspired widespread protests at home, particularly among the young. Vietnam protests had in fact turned violent by 1968, and Nixon worried they would become a threat to civil order. Nixon's plan for Vietnam, which he and his advisers developed over time as new events unfolded, was to tone down protests at home while withdrawing American ground troops. At the same time, however, Nixon did not want to appear to be conceding defeat in Vietnam, and on numerous occasions he did not hesitate to demonstrate American air power. As Nixon himself put it, what he sought in Vietnam was "peace with honor."

As a candidate in 1968, Nixon had told Americans that he would end the war quickly after he entered office. However, he had no specific plan for carrying this out. In the terms of the day he was a pro-war "hawk" rather than a peace-seeking "dove," and he had criticized Lyndon Johnson for not using greater force. By the time he became president, however, Nixon knew he could not allow the war to drag on. The costs were too high, for one thing. By 1969 there had been 31,000 U.S. casualties, and men were still dying at the rate of two hundred per week. Beyond that, Vietnam was costing America $30 billion per year. Also, Nixon felt threatened by ongoing antiwar protests. The president was determined to get the United States out of the war at the least cost to the nation and himself; at the same time, he wanted America to remain strong rather than appear to be the loser in the conflict.

Nixon's first step was to implement a policy known as Vietnamization. The policy, announced at a meeting with South Vietnamese leader Nguyen Van Thieu in June 1969, was designed to give responsibility for the conflict to Thieu and his armies. On the one hand, Americans continued to train and arm the South Vietnamese. On the other, Nixon began the pullback of American troops in a program of "phased withdrawal," which was largely complete by August 1972.

Vietnamization was also directed at the Soviet Union and China. Nixon hoped it would inspire the Soviets to bring pressure on the North Vietnamese to negotiate. The Chinese, for their part, waited until troop withdrawals began to begin serious talks about normalizing diplomatic relations.

Nixon's decision to bomb Cambodia in the spring of 1969, however, made Vietnamization an inconsistent policy, as the bombing seemed like a move to expand the Vietnam War rather than bring it to an end. The bombing was an attack on "sanctuaries" the North Vietnamese had established in Cambodia, from which they were making attacks on South Vietnam.

Nixon and Kissinger decided to keep the bombing of the Cambodian sanctuaries, illegal since Cambodia was a noncombatant, secret from the American public. This required the manipulation and falsification of military records. Reports of the bombing were eventually leaked, however, and published in the *New York Times*, although not many paid attention to the reports at first. Angered, Nixon began to use wiretaps in order to prevent further leaks.

The next year, Nixon found a second opportunity to expand the conflict, rendering Vietnamization even more problematic. Cambodia's Prince Norodom Sihanouk, neutral in the conflicts raging nearby, was overthrown by the anti-Communist general Lon Nol. North Vietnam launched an immediate attack on Cambodia. Nixon was as unwilling to accept a military defeat in Cambodia as he was in South Vietnam. Consequently, he authorized extensive American support for an invasion of Cambodia by South Vietnam. The invasion of Cambodia inspired some of the largest antiwar protests of the era. Americans from all walks of life opposed the invasion, and many accused Nixon of being a liar and hypocrite; it seemed he wanted to broaden the Vietnam War rather than end it. In retaliation, Nixon referred to some student protestors as "bums." By the middle of May 1970, tensions were so high that students were killed, accidentally, at Kent State and Jackson State Universities.

Nixon had always believed that antiwar protestors were a small, if noisy, minority. He placed his faith in what he called, in contrast, the "silent majority." They were the larger group of Americans who did not stage protests, take over buildings on college campuses, or threaten, as Nixon saw it, the stability of America. They certainly did not attract media attention. Nixon believed that the silent majority who had elected him shared his attitudes and goals, particularly in making a strong stand in Vietnam. However, in the uproar after the Cambodian invasion, even many of the silent majority spoke out against Nixon's decision. Congress responded by denying funding for further American action in Cambodia, at least for a time. Nixon soon realized he could not have it both ways; he could no longer pursue both the withdrawal of troops and an escalation of the war involving American ground forces.

An alternative was to improve the fighting ability of the South Vietnamese, in the plan that became Vietnamization. In February 1971, an opportunity to test their ability came when a large South Vietnamese force, supported by American supplies and intelligence, entered yet another neighboring country, Laos. The invasion of Laos was intended to interrupt the so-called Ho Chi Minh Trail, which connected North Vietnam with its sympathizers in the south. The trail ran through parts of both Cambodia and Laos, and provided for the movement of troops and supplies. Like the invasion of Cambodia the year before, the incursion into Laos was a failure, and it sparked more opposition to Nixon's Vietnam policy at home.

Negotiations and American Air Power

Despite these setbacks, which brought Vietnamization effectively to an end, Nixon continued troop withdrawals and sought to negotiate peace terms with the North Vietnamese. The negotiations themselves, which were largely conducted in Paris between Kissinger and North Vietnamese negotiator Le Duc Tho, went very slowly. Nixon demanded the preservation of an independent South Vietnam under Thieu while the North Vietnamese wanted to reunite the country under their authority. Another of Nixon's problems, antiwar protests at home, were less of a threat to Nixon by the end of 1971. They grew less widespread and less vocal as greater numbers of American troops came home. Nixon's September 1971 decision to end the draft also helped address many protestors' concerns.

Nixon found new opportunities to use American force in the period from late 1971 until the official cease-fire took effect on January 27, 1973. In this period, however, Nixon replaced American ground troops and support for South Vietnamese forces with air power. Late in 1971, North Vietnamese forces launched a largely successful offensive against the south. Soon, they were confident of total victory and not inclined to negotiate. Nixon reacted strongly. On May 8, 1972, in a move which earlier leaders and Nixon himself had avoided, the president authorized the mining of the harbor at Haiphong, North Vietnam's main port, as well as other ports. In addition, he began an extensive bombing campaign against North Vietnamese cities, particularly the capital, Hanoi. Between May and

October 1972 more than 41,000 bombing missions were launched against North Vietnam.

Again protestors spoke out against this new escalation. Many were offended by the fact that the bombings were attacks on the people of North Vietnam as opposed to its army. Protests, however, remained small. Instead, polls indicated that once again Nixon had the silent majority behind him. Many Americans approved of Nixon's decision to use America's greatest and most decisive military advantage, overwhelming air power, to finally end the Vietnam War.

Urged on by the Soviets and the Chinese, and certain that Nixon would be re-elected in 1972 (and then become more stubborn), North Vietnamese negotiators returned to the bargaining table in the autumn of 1972. On October 12, Kissinger and Le Duc Tho reached what were later termed the Paris Peace Accords, which decreed a cease-fire in Vietnam, the withdrawal of American troops, and, to the dismay of South Vietnamese leaders, an official recognition of the Vietcong as a legitimate political force. Worse, as far as South Vietnamese president Thieu was concerned, the North Vietnamese army would remain in the south. Not surprisingly, Thieu expressed his objections to the Paris Accords strongly. Kissinger passed the objections on to the North Vietnamese, who took the opportunity to once again stall negotiations.

On December 16 negotiations collapsed, and Nixon responded with yet another display of American air power: the Christmas bombing of 1972. Except on Christmas Day itself, as many as 120 air strikes a day were launched against North Vietnam. The costs were high. In addition to many North Vietnamese civilian deaths, ninety-three American flyers went missing. Protestors again criticized Nixon's attempt to bomb North Vietnam "back to the stone age," as the president put it, but shortly thereafter, North Vietnamese leaders agreed to abide by the Paris Accords. When the cease-fire took effect on January 27, 1973, American involvement in the Vietnam War officially came to an end.

Nixon's administration had, in its haphazard way, extricated the United States from a conflict which had cost 57,000 American lives (as well as untold Southeast Asian ones). Whether it was a peace with honor, however, remains a subject for debate. Nixon and Kissinger made a secret pledge to return American forces to Vietnam if Thieu was endangered by the north. But after the last American troops came home in March 1973, Vietnam was largely forgotten. After Nixon resigned from office, the north completed its conquest of the south. Saigon, the South Vietnamese capital, fell on April 30, 1975.

The Background to Watergate

Nixon's emphasis on centralized authority allowed him to accomplish a great deal in foreign as well as domestic policy. This approach, however, also worked against him. Nixon's over-reliance on loyal advisers, combined with his own disregard for governmental checks and balances, helped to bring about the scandal which ended his presidency. Regardless of détente and the opening of China and despite certain innovative domestic reforms, what most people associate with Nixon's presidency is the Watergate scandal.

Watergate ultimately ended Nixon's presidency. Two years of investigations made it clear that Nixon was guilty of various abuses of presidential power as well as obstruction of justice, and he chose to resign rather than face impeachment. Perhaps, however, Watergate was an accident waiting to happen.

Nixon began using political "dirty tricks," as they were eventually dubbed, early in his presidency. From the beginning he was concerned about information leaks, believing they threatened both his political standing and the welfare of the country. In order to stop leaks, Nixon did not hesitate to employ special investigations, wiretaps, lie detector tests, and even legal proceedings. Even his staff members, from whom Nixon expected unquestioned loyalty, were subject to the president's paranoia about leaks. To make matters worse, Nixon grew to distrust governmental intelligence agencies such as the FBI or CIA; as was his general practice, Nixon left information-gathering and leak-plugging to his close aides.

In the spring of 1969, news of the secret bombing of Cambodia was leaked to a reporter for the *New York Times*, who published details of the supposedly covert bombing. Nixon and Kissinger were so angry they began to order wiretaps on certain reporters and government officials. In some cases these wiretaps were illegal.

Leaks, however, continued, as did the Nixon administration's strong reactions to them. In June 1971, the *New York Times* began to publish parts of what eventually became known as the Pentagon Papers. These were reports on the origins and expansion of the Vietnam War assembled by the Department of Defense (DOD) which were leaked by former DOD employee Daniel Ellsberg. The papers detailed how the government, during Johnson's administration, had misled the public about the war in Vietnam.

Although the Pentagon Papers did not implicate Nixon directly, he was furious that they had been leaked. He believed such reports should be censored for the sake of national security. To try to stop continued publication of the Pentagon Papers, Nixon went to court, a battle he ultimately lost. More tellingly for the future, Nixon and his advisers decided to attack the credibility of Daniel Ellsberg.

The Plumbers

To do this, Nixon's team needed damaging information on Ellsberg. They used a special investigative unit within the White House to collect the information. The unit was known, since it was formed to stop leaks, as the Plumbers.

Although the idea behind the Plumbers came from the highest levels within the White House (Kissinger, Haldeman, Ehrlichman, and Nixon himself), low-level staffers without intelligence-gathering experience were recruited to organize the Plumbers. Among the important Plumbers were Chuck Colson, a White House lawyer, and Egil "Bud" Krogh, a member of Ehrlichman's staff. What they lacked in experience they made up in a more important quality: loyalty to Nixon.

The leaders of the Plumbers realized they needed men with relevant experience in covert operations to assist them. They hired G. Gordon Liddy, counsel to the Committee to Re-elect the President (CRP, or, to Nixon's enemies, CREEP), and E. Howard Hunt, a former CIA agent with connections to anti-Communist Cubans. Colson, Liddy, and Hunt devised a plan to collect damaging information on Ellsberg by breaking into the office of Ellsberg's psychiatrist in Los Angeles. The first of the illegal break-ins, the precursor to Watergate, took place on September 4, 1971.

The success of the Ellsberg break-in, perhaps, emboldened the Plumbers. On March 30, 1972, a meeting took place involving, among others, Jeb Magruder, the assistant director of CRP, John Mitchell, wearing two hats as the director of CRP and attorney general, and Liddy, who had concocted an elaborate and expensive intelligence-gathering program. Mitchell allegedly approved $250,000 for Liddy's plan, which included a break-in at Democratic National Headquarters in the Watergate office and apartment complex in Washington, D.C.

Therefore, the scandal that ended Nixon's presidency began with what his press secretary, Ron Ziegler, referred to as a "third-rate burglary." On May 27, 1972, and again on June 17, five men broke into the headquarters of the Democratic National Committee (DNC) , which was in the Watergate building. The second time they were arrested by local police. The five burglars were found photographing documents and planting listening devices, or bugs. Their leader, James McCord, was the security director of CRP. The other burglars were some of Hunt's Cubans.

Nixon, at that time on a brief holiday in Key Biscayne, Florida, read about the break-in the next morning, June 18, in a local newspaper. He did not believe the crime had any connection to him, and the consensus is that Nixon knew nothing about the original break-in. In fact, at the time, Nixon could not understand what advantage was to be gained by breaking into DNC headquarters. Nixon had no problem with illicitly-obtained political information; he simply did not believe there was any valuable information to be found in the Watergate offices.

Investigators soon connected the five Watergate burglars with White House staffers Liddy and Hunt. Liddy, Hunt, McCord, and the four others were indicted by a grand jury under federal judge John Sirica.

The Watergate Cover-Up

The scandal had only just begun, however, with the indictment of the Watergate burglars. Nixon was first informed of a possible White House connection to the break-in as early as June 20, 1972, and he urged chief of staff Haldeman to keep him informed. On June 23, in a taped conversation with Haldeman, the president approved a plan to interfere with the Watergate investigation, which was then being conducted by the FBI. Nixon told Haldeman that political pressure should be brought to bear on acting FBI director Patrick Gray to stop the investigation. Nixon was afraid that information damaging to his presidential campaign might be revealed.

In this instance, Nixon was in fact using the authority of his office to obstruct justice by interfering with a criminal investigation. Other accusations were to be leveled against the president over the next two years, and only when the tape of the June 23 conversation was finally released in the summer of 1974 would Nixon's accusers claim they had found the "smoking gun" that proved Nixon guilty of obstruction of justice.

In the summer and fall of 1972, however, Nixon had no idea how persistent Watergate investigators would prove to be. Judge Sirica thought that the break-in went deeper than the original seven burglars. He strongly urged them to speak up on their ties to the White House. During the same period, reporters for the *Washington Post* began their own investigation of the case. Nixon himself, in the face of mounting curiosity from Sirica and the press, ordered an in-house investigation. He said he wanted to find out whether, and to what extent, White House staffers were involved in Watergate.

In the meantime, Nixon enjoyed a landslide victory over his democratic opponent, George McGovern, in the 1972 election. He considered the huge margin of victory to be a sign of approval from the American public, as well as a mandate to pursue his domestic and foreign agendas.

Watergate, however, returned to haunt Nixon; it soon made it difficult for him to pursue any agenda aside from political survival. In March 1973, McCord claimed in a note to Sirica that White House officials had offered payoffs and other favors to Watergate defendants in return for their silence. This was the first real hint that high-level Nixon administration staffers, and perhaps Nixon himself, were involved in a cover-up over Watergate. Soon, a special Senate Watergate committee, chaired by Sam Ervin of North Carolina, was investigating Watergate in addition to Sirica's grand jury and the Washington press.

Nixon's aides began to desert him. Some acted out of fear of prosecution, others out of the concern that they might be blamed for the entire scandal. Jeb Magruder, the deputy chairman of CRP and therefore a relatively minor administration official, claimed that Mitchell had approved the Watergate break-in. A higher-level official, special White House counsel John Dean, began to bargain with prosecutors in order to deflect the blame away from himself. Dean testified in grand jury hearings that, among others, Haldeman and Ehrlichman were involved in the cover-up. Nixon, in his own attempts to keep the presidency free of the scandal, asked for and received the resignations of Haldeman, Ehrlichman, and Dean by the end of April 1973.

In nationally televised hearings in front of Ervin's Senate committee, Dean later implicated Nixon himself. He said that Nixon had claimed he would have no problem raising money to pay off the original Watergate burglars. Dean went on to add that Nixon's offenses might go beyond the Watergate cover-up itself to other examples of presidential dirty tricks, such as Nixon's so-called "enemies list" which contained the names of people the administration was to target with wiretappings, tax audits, and other dubious actions.

The Tapes and the Saturday Night Massacre

Not long after Dean's testimony, on July 16, 1973, an aide revealed that Nixon had tape-recorded most of his White House conversations. The tapes were immediately subpoenaed by Watergate investigators, but Nixon refused to turn them over. He claimed executive privilege, meaning in this case that the president had special rights with regard to his privacy. He argued that the tapes might reveal crucial information that would compromise both his presidency and national security.

In addition to Sirica and Ervin, the tapes were also requested by Archibald Cox, a special Watergate prosecutor appointed by attorney general Elliot Richardson (Mitchell and a successor, Richard Kleindienst, had since resigned). In October, Nixon responded to Cox's repeated demands for the tapes by having him fired. Also dismissed was deputy attorney general William Ruckelshaus. Richardson resigned in protest. This event, the so-called "Saturday night massacre," left more and more people thinking

Nixon had something to hide. They also began to wonder why he felt so free in abusing presidential authority. In the aftermath of the Saturday night massacre, a new special prosecutor was appointed. He was Leon Jaworski, a Texas attorney Nixon believed would be sympathetic to him.

Events, however, soon made much sympathy on Jaworski's part difficult. The various investigations, inspired partly by Dean's testimony, began to turn up new administration scandals. John Ehrlichman, for instance, was indicted for his involvement in the illegal break-in at Ellsberg's psychiatrist's office. Nixon's vice president, Spiro Agnew, was forced to resign in order to avoid prosecution for charges including bribery and tax fraud. Nixon himself was investigated for misusing funds and for not paying his taxes. The press, the public, and even certain members of Congress began to call for Nixon to resign or face impeachment. Nixon, more and more embattled, proclaimed famously, "I am not a crook." His denial did little to convince people. The House of Representatives, on October 30, 1973, began impeachment investigations.

Continued Denials

Nixon continued denying any involvement in Watergate. At the very least, he did not cooperate with investigators. In the worst scenario, Nixon actively used his presidential authority to obstruct justice. After a public outcry, Nixon finally began surrendering tapes to investigators. Some of the tapes however, had been tampered with. There were gaps that experts soon determined to be intentional erasures. Nixon remained combative through the winter and spring of 1974. He claimed at various points that he did not expect to be impeached, and that he had no intention of resigning.

However, matters continued to worsen. In February 1974, Sirica's grand jury named him an "unindicted co-conspirator" in the Watergate break-in. This meant that

Richard Nixon resigned from office to avoid impeachment. Here, on his final day as president, he is accompanied by his wife Pat, Vice-President Gerald Ford, and Mrs. Betty Ford.

Nixon was susceptible to criminal charges. In coming months, the calls for the tapes continued from the grand jury, from the Senate committee, and now from the House impeachment committee. Nixon released more of the tapes, but only grudgingly and slowly.

Resignation and Exile

The end of Nixon's presidency finally came with two developments. The first was the decision by the United States Supreme Court that Nixon could no longer hide behind executive privilege; he had to release all of his tapes to Leon Jaworski. One of the newly released tapes provided investigators with a "smoking gun": It proved that Nixon had been involved in the Watergate cover-up as early as June 23, 1972, only six days after the original burglars were captured. Nixon could be heard on the tapes urging that political pressure be put on FBI and CIA officials to stop the Watergate investigation.

On July 30, 1974, the second development took place. The House Judiciary Committee approved three articles of impeachment against the president. He was charged with obstruction of justice, abuse of presidential powers, and interfering with the impeachment process itself. Nixon faced being tried publicly by Congress, and, if found guilty, forcibly removed from office to perhaps face criminal charges.

Knowing that he stood little chance of surviving impeachment hearings, Nixon chose to resign as president effective August 9, 1974.

Nixon's successor, Gerald Ford, later pardoned him of all criminal wrongdoing in connection with Watergate. Nonetheless, his political career ended in scandal and disgrace. In the eyes of the public, Nixon remained guilty of obstruction of justice, abuse of presidential power, and perhaps most significantly for his reputation, consistent lies and amoral behavior.

After his retirement, Nixon spent his time writing his memoirs and other books. He enjoyed a brief rehabilitation of his reputation in the mid-1980s, particularly as a foreign policy expert. On April 22, 1994, Richard Nixon passed away. He is buried in Yorba Linda, California.

CHAPTER

1

NIXON AND THE ENVIRONMENTAL MOVEMENT

Nixon: A Reluctant Environmentalist

Charles S. Warren

When Richard Nixon first took office in 1969, pressure to enact environmental protections was mounting on both Congress and the president himself. Nixon responded with the passage of the National Environmental Policy Act of 1969 and the creation of the Environmental Protection Agency (EPA) in 1970.

In the following selection, excerpted from a speech given at a conference at Hofstra University in 1987, Charles S. Warren claims that Nixon should not be given too much credit for the environmental accomplishments of his presidency. Warren notes that the Nixon administration gave the EPA much less power than it could have. In addition, Nixon created the Office of Management and Budget, which could interfere with environmental actions on grounds of expense. Moreover, Warren contends, Nixon himself was not very interested in the environment. Warren is an environmental lawyer at the firm of Berle, Kass, and Case in New York City. In the 1970s he was a regional administrator for the United States Environmental Protection Agency.

THE ADMINISTRATION OF RICHARD NIXON IS NOT GENERALLY remembered as one that stood for strong environmental protection, and certainly protection of the environment was not a major interest of that administration. However, tremendous progress was made during the administration in attempting to clean up the air and water

Excerpted from *Richard M. Nixon: Politician, President, Administrator*, edited by Leon Friedman and William F. Levantrosser. Copyright ©1991 by Hofstra University. Reproduced by permission of Greenwood Publishing Group, Inc., Westport, Conn.

and in raising the public's consciousness with regard to the issue of environmental protection. . . .

The Establishment of EPA and Other Administrative Reforms

Perhaps the greatest environmental achievement of the Nixon Administration was the creation of the Environmental Protection Agency (EPA) in 1970. Before there was an EPA, federal environmental programs were scattered around in a number of agencies, such as the Departments of Interior, of Health, Education, and Welfare (HEW), and of Agriculture; the Corps of Engineers; and others. There was in no sense a focused federal approach to environmental problems.

In early 1970, the president's Advisory Council on Executive Organization recommended a series of reorganization plans, which affected most of the government. In the environmental area, the council recommended that a new department called Natural Resources and the Environment be created, which would sweep all the environmental programs into one massive entity. This proposal, as well as most of the reorganization proposals, ran into tremendous opposition in Congress and within the administration itself. With regard to the Department of Natural Resources and the Environment, many in Congress felt that environmental programs would be submerged in a big department where there would be conflicting programmatic and budgetary priorities. There was also concern that combining developmental activities, such as initiating water resource projects and leasing federal lands, and environmental protection activities in one department would lead to conflicts that would not benefit environmental programs. Inside the administration, the secretaries of HEW, commerce, and agriculture were protesting against losing authority to the Interior Department, which would be a major effect of the reorganization plan.

As a result of the opposition from Congress and from

forces within the administration, the reorganization plan for a new Department of Natural Resources and Environment was not pursued by the administration, and a more modest proposal was sent to the Congress to create the EPA. This new plan took effect on December 2, 1970, and established an agency that for the first time could take a coordinated approach to environmental problems. . . .

Placing all of the major environmental functions in the new agency allowed for the development of a committed group of people whose job was to focus on the environment and do something about the problems of air pollution, water pollution, solid and hazardous waste, and pesticides. Certainly in its early years, EPA was a vigorous agency, which set standards and implemented the new laws passed by Congress in an aggressive manner. The Nixon Administration deserves credit for establishing the EPA and also for choosing as its first two administrators, William D. Ruckelshaus and Russell E. Train. Both of these administrators proved to be strong leaders who were able to stand up to major industries, such as the auto and steel industries, and also to the forces within the Nixon Administration itself who attempted to weaken certain of the early regulations. It was extremely important that EPA get off to a good start, and the appointments of Ruckelshaus, who served from the beginning of the EPA until April 1973, and his successor Train, who served until the end of 1976, enabled EPA to establish itself as an effective environmental agency. . . .

The Legislative Explosion

There had certainly been legislation passed by Congress before 1969 to deal with environmental problems, and some limited progress had been made by 1969 in developing approaches to controlling air and water pollution. Unfortunately, most of the laws did not give the federal government authority to effectively deal with national problems, such as air and water pollution, which had elicited great concern on the part of many Americans. The beginning of the Nixon Administration coincided with Congressional efforts, led by such senators as Edmund Muskie of Maine and Henry Jackson of Washington, to significantly strengthen federal environmental laws.

The first major legislation passed by Congress during the Nixon Administration was the National Environmental Policy Act [NEPA] of 1969. This was largely a congressional initiative, and it brought about a fundamental change in the way federal agencies did business. In its most significant section, it required all agencies of the federal government to include in every recommendation or report on proposals for legislation and other major federal actions a detailed statement of the environmental impact of the proposed action and a discussion of alternatives and the adverse environmental effects that cannot be avoided if the proposal is implemented. In one short section of the law, the famous environmental impact statement was born. For the first time, federal agencies were required to consider and disclose the environmental impacts of their decisions and actions. Over the years since the enactment of NEPA, the courts have made the environmental impact statement requirement one of the most important tools in the arsenal of those who seek to delay, change, or stop government actions that may adversely affect the environment. Following passage of the federal law, many states passed their own equivalent of NEPA so that actions of state agencies would also be given similar scrutiny with regard to environmental effects. NEPA was a landmark law that was not initiated by the Nixon administration, but the administration supported it and helped implement the law in its beginning stages.

Shortly after signing NEPA into law, President Nixon's State of the Union address on January 22, 1970, devoted several pages to environmental protection and helped set the stage for an active legislative year. This was followed by

Environmentalism Is a Fad

Former Nixon speechwriter William Safire remembered that he and his colleagues believed that public interest in the environment would fade away.

None of us doubted that the environment issue, which had been captured by faddists and turned into an unassailable crusade by editorial writers, would be abandoned by all of them as soon as something sexier came along—leaving the Nixon Administration to carry the fight in the face of growing opposition from consumers (pollution devices drove up prices) and labor. Carry the good fight on against pollution we would, doing what was right to clean up the air and water, feeling sorry for ourselves all the way as the fashionable-issue set traipsed off with public attention on some fresh, newsworthy endeavor.

William Safire, *Before the Fall: An Inside View of the Pre-Watergate White House.* New York: Doubleday, 1975.

the President's Message on the Environment, issued February 10, 1970, detailing a number of proposals that helped lay the groundwork for subsequent congressional action.

The Environmental Message recommended a new $4 billion federal plan for construction of waste treatment plants to control water pollution, a number of changes in water quality standards, and the strengthening of federal enforcement mechanisms in severe water pollution emergencies. While these measures were not revolutionary, and stopped well short of future congressional action in 1972, they were a sign of increased federal attention to the problems of water pollution.

The message also called for a number of new initiatives

to help clean up the air. These included more stringent automobile standards, testing of representative cars off the assembly line, regulation of fuel composition and additives, and establishment of nationwide air quality standards and state plans to implement those standards. This clearly signaled administration support for comprehensive revision of the federal Clean Air Act.

After a lengthy congressional debate and against strong industry opposition, the Clean Air Amendments of 1970 were signed into law on December 31, 1970. The new law represented the most controversial and far-reaching effort to control air pollution attempted in this country. . . .

The President's Message on the Environment in 1971 also contained a number of new environmental initiatives. Besides repeating certain parts of his air and water pollution programs, the message also suggested new proposals for the registration of pesticides, restrictions on the use of toxic substances, a new program for control of ocean dumping, and a new program for noise control. The message also called for a controversial national land use policy.

The next series of major legislative actions occurred in 1972 when a great number of new laws were passed to deal with a number of environmental problems. The most important of these was the Federal Water Pollution Control Act of 1972. This law, which was the culmination of a long debate in the Congress, made radical changes in the way water pollution problems were handled in the United States. The law established a new national goal of the elimination of discharge of pollutants into navigable waters. . . .

Questions About Nixon's Commitment to the Environment

Even though the Nixon Administration had supported a number of strong environmental measures, there were legitimate questions raised as to the strength of the administration's commitment and whether its activities were dictated purely by a desire to ride the wave of public opinion in support of the environment in the early 1970s. There is no doubt that credit must be given for support of measures like the Clean Air Act, for administrative actions such as the creation of EPA, and for a series of strong environmental messages that were issued in 1970 and 1971. However, a number of incidents starting in 1971 raised serious questions about the administration's true support for the environment.

Most glaring was the attempt by Peter Flanigan, a key member of the White House staff, to interfere in the Armco Steel case when it was subject to a court enforcement proceeding. Flanigan attempted to pressure EPA into settling the case on terms more favorable to the company, after receiving a letter from the company president. This attempt failed, but it should never have received such high-level attention, and the effort to interfere in an enforcement proceeding before a court was extremely troubling.

An even more far-reaching effort was made by the Office of Management and Budget (OMB), which had been established in the office of the president in 1969 to coordinate a review of EPA regulations. The review would involve other agencies who could raise objections to particular regulations in order to persuade EPA to change those regulations. This issue came up again and again throughout the administration, and there were attempts to weaken a number of regulations under the Clean Air Act. Congress held hearings on this process with regard to regulations setting requirements for state implementation plans, and EPA successfully resisted the pressure from OMB. The issue came up again with regard to phasing out lead in gasoline and in the case of a requested delay by the auto companies in the timetable for meeting standards. EPA again successfully resisted this type of interference, but did modify the final lead phasedown to some extent.

Both William Ruckelshaus and Russell Train had to

fight numerous battles to keep EPA regulations from being weakened as a result of this review process. The danger in such a procedure is that it gives industry and others a separate avenue outside of the public process to pursue their own point of view. All parties can be heard in the public process, and then EPA can issue its final regulations. The OMB process allows a small group of government officials, who are usually concerned about the economic effect of a particular regulation, to argue their case in private. Unfortunately, the OMB review started in the Nixon Administration has now become firmly imbedded by the Reagan Administration, with the result that it is very difficult for EPA to put out strong regulations under any of its statutes.

Another confrontation between the White House and EPA took place in early 1974, when there was pressure on EPA to submit amendments weakening the Clean Air Act to Congress because of the oil crises brought on by the 1973 Middle East war. Russell Train had to threaten to resign in order to get the White House to pull back from its original proposals. This demonstrated that significant forces within the administration were prepared to weaken environmental laws in the name of energy conservation before there was any evidence that such steps were necessary or would help alleviate the energy problem. . . .

Nixon's Mixed Legacy

Looking back at the Nixon Administration's environmental record, it is apparent that it was a mixed record with quite a few positive developments and some negative aspects. Richard Nixon never demonstrated that he had a deep personal commitment to the environment. However, in the beginning of his administration, he obviously heard the public outcry for stronger laws and reacted to that spur. He also surrounded himself with strong environmental leaders, such as Russell Train and William Ruckelshaus who were able to advance the cause quite significantly in those early years. Toward the end of the administration, when the public outcry had become somewhat muted and other concerns had arisen, such as the oil crises, there was a considerable erosion in the administration's support of environmental issues. That change, coupled with the insertion of OMB into EPA's regulation process, dims some of the luster of the Nixon environmental record.

However, on balance, the efforts of the administration in the beginning years were crucial to seeing that EPA got off to a good start and that progress was made in passing new laws to deal with a great many environmental problems. A review of the entire Nixon Administration record leads one to come out on the positive side of the ledger and to favorably compare that administration's record with those of succeeding administrations of both parties.

THE NIXON ADMINISTRATION RESPONDED QUICKLY TO ENVIRONMENTAL CONCERNS

JOHN C. WHITAKER

In this selection from his book on environmental policy during the presidencies of Richard Nixon and Gerald Ford, John C. Whitaker argues that Nixon should be praised for acting aggressively in response to the concerns of the environmental movement. In the summer of 1969, following the recommendations of aides such as John Ehrlichman, Nixon set up an environmental task force to shape the administration's approach. Whitaker served as leader of that task force.

In late November 1969, Whitaker's group provided Nixon with guidelines for his developing environmental policy. They included the establishment of the Environmental Protection Agency, specific measures to address air and water pollution, an emphasis on cleaning up federal facilities, and an effort to establish more public parks. The author describes how Nixon had to act within the limitations of real-world politics and budgets. Whitaker was a deputy assistant to Nixon and later served as undersecretary of the Department of the Interior.

THERE IS STILL ONLY ONE WORD, *HYSTERIA*, TO DESCRIBE THE Washington mood on the environment issue in the fall of 1969. The words *pollution* and *environment* were on every politician's lips. The press gave the issue extraordinary

Excerpted from *Striking a Balance: Environment and Natural Resources Policy in the Nixon-Ford Years*, by John C. Whitaker. Copyright ©1976 by American Enterprise Institute for Public Policy Research, Washington, D.C. Reprinted with permission.

coverage, Congress responded by producing environment-related bills by the bushel, and the President was in danger of being left behind.

On May 29, 1969, Nixon announced the formation of a cabinet committee called the Environmental Quality Council. Dr. Lee DuBridge, science adviser to the President, was named executive secretary, and the staff to support the cabinet committee was provided by the Office of Science and Technology, which DuBridge also directed.

Nixon held cabinet meetings on such subjects as pesticides, outdoor recreation, air pollution standards, and development of a low-pollution unconventional automobile engine. But the meetings left him dissatisfied. There was too much scientific jargon. Only bits and pieces of issues were tossed at him. There was no overall strategy. Should enforcement be by regulation, or by user fees, or a combination of both? What were the overall costs to industry and the consumer, in terms of the increased price of products for various pollution abatement schedules under varying standards and regulations? Finally, what effects would the various clean-up scenarios have upon the federal budget? None of these fundamental questions was being answered....

The President's Environmental Message Task Force

The author did not put together the environment task force, he inherited one, a very good one. The credit should go to Egil Krogh, who handled the environment issue under [presidential advisor John] Ehrlichman for the President briefly in the summer of 1969, when it became apparent to Nixon that neither the cabinet committee nor the staff of the Office of Science and Technology was progressing on the issue to his satisfaction. The author took over leadership of the task force in late August 1969. Its members were bright and young, with the stamina routinely to put in twelve- to fourteen-hour days....

By the long Thanksgiving weekend in November 1969, the task force was able to supply President Nixon with a sixty-five-page outline of preliminary recommendations for his environmental message to Congress, scheduled for early February 1970. Mr. Nixon studied the recommendations over the weekend at Key Biscayne, scribbled marginal notes, and gave the task force its first guidance. Five major areas were covered in the report.

Creation of the EPA

1. A New Department of Environment and Natural Resources. President Nixon was acutely aware of the extent to which responsibility for the environment was dispersed throughout the government. At cabinet meetings he had watched Secretary Robert H. Finch at Health, Education, and Welfare (HEW) and Secretary John A. Volpe at the Department of Transportation (DOT) argue over which department should take the lead in developing an unconventional low-polluting automobile. On pesticides, Secretary Walter J. Hickel at Interior and Secretary Finch at HEW had argued for tighter pesticide controls, while Secretary Clifford M. Hardin at Agriculture emphasized the increased crop productivity resulting from the application of pesticides. . . . And so it went. There was hardly a cabinet officer around the table who did not have a stake in the pollution issue. Even the postmaster general joined the debate, offering to use postal cars to test an experimental fleet of low-pollution vehicles.

The task force report to the President highlighted the problem of fragmented responsibility.

> The federal government spends billions of dollars annually on programs to protect or enhance the environment. It spends billions more on activities which are not so designed but which nonetheless have profound environmental consequences (highways and location of

federal facilities, for example). Yet there is no single member of the President's Cabinet with responsibility for the environment, and programs are dispersed almost haphazardly among the departments. In recent years the Secretary of the Interior has become de facto Secretary of the Environment, yet these concerns have not penetrated far into the Department—beyond the Secretary's Office. At any rate, he does not have control over many of the most important environmental programs, and he has many unrelated responsibilities.

. . . A truly comprehensive department would include the Forest Service from the Department of Agriculture and the Corps of (Civil) Engineers from the Department of Defense, both politically sensitive agencies with powerful and possessive congressional patrons. A less politically risky alternative was offered to Nixon—"at a minimum, the name of the Department of Interior could be changed and its statement of purposes revised, the Bureau of Indian Affairs transferred to HEW, and the Air Pollution Control Administration transferred to the new department." But Nixon scribbled "good idea" next to the full Department of Environment and Natural Resources option, thus signaling that he was prepared to take the political heat. Later the concept was altered: an Environmental Protection Agency and a Department of Natural Resources were proposed, and the idea of a Department of Environmental and Natural Resources was dropped.

Reducing Air and Water Pollution

2. Air Pollution. President Nixon agreed to a recommendation to begin federal development and procurement of unconventionally powered low-pollution experimental automobiles. The task force advised him that, given available and foreseeable technology, automotive emissions could be reduced gradually until the late 1970s and early 1980s, but that thereafter, barring unforeseen developments in the internal combustion engine, total emissions would begin to increase again because of the increased numbers of vehicles in use. In the cabinet, Transportation Secretary John Volpe, Health, Education, and Welfare Secretary Robert Finch and Science Adviser Lee DuBridge all backed the program, but Nixon had doubts. He believed the federal effort would lack the technical competence and funds that Detroit could bring to bear to solve the problem. Besides, he was fed up with the infighting to control the proposed program between Finch, whose department had authority to set auto emission standards, and Volpe, whose department already had a program to design experimental cars to improve safety and study alternative power sources. But the task force's view—ultimately accepted by Nixon—was that, left to itself, the automobile industry was unlikely, because of its enormous investment in the internal combustion engine, to make a heavy investment in alternative low-pollution power sources. So, an outside force was needed to demonstrate to the public that a very low-pollution vehicle was possible. Finally, federal sponsorship might stimulate commercial production of such vehicles in competition with the existing automobile industry. . . .

3. *Water Pollution.* The task force pointed out that, unlike the situation in air pollution where the technology was lacking to reduce auto emissions and to lower sulfur dioxides in fossil fuels, no technological breakthroughs were required to clean up the nation's waters. All that was needed was money, huge amounts of it. In the four years since the Clean Waters Restoration Act of 1966, federal appropriations for constructing municipal treatment plants had totaled only about one-third of authorizations. Not until fiscal year (FY) 1970 had federal funding taken any major leap upward—from $214 million to $800 million. The report argued that much more money was needed. It recommended an investment of about $10 billion in federal, state and local funds over a five-year period, to be provided ei-

ther by increasing appropriations in the existing grant program or, as Secretary Hickel wanted, through federal contracting authority in the amount of $10 billion to repay the principal on municipal bonds sold to finance waste treatment plants. . . .

Most fundamental of all, [the task force recommended] taking action to increase and speed up enforcement powers against polluters. As in the case of air pollution, the task force reported that the states had little incentive, except for public opinion, to stop water pollution. They would have to impose large costs on local governments and industries. Industries could pack up and take their payrolls and taxes elsewhere if strong standards were enforced. Also, states were timid about enforcing tough water pollution standards on large interstate rivers and lakes unless they were sure that other states bordering the same waters had similar standards. As the President later put it in his environmental message to Congress: "As controls over interstate waters are tightened, polluting industries will be increasingly tempted to locate on intrastate lakes and rivers—with a consequently increased threat to those waterways—unless they, too, are brought under the same strictures. I propose . . . a simple but profoundly significant principle: that the nation's waterways belong to all of us, and that neither a municipality nor an industry should be allowed to discharge wastes into those waterways beyond their capacity to absorb the wastes without becoming polluted."

But the federal government's ability to take action was not much better than that of the states. Federal enforcement was impossibly cumbersome. First, the secretary of the interior had to call conferences and hearings and wait one year before he could request the attorney general to bring suit to secure a pollution abatement schedule. Even then, any industry or municipality with reasonably competent legal help could stall on a cease-and-desist order for months, even years, knowing that an ultimate contempt-of-court citation was a minor inconvenience compared to the cost of installing the pollution abatement equipment needed to comply with water quality standards.

The task force recommended, and Nixon agreed to, quicker enforcement actions, including fines up to $10,000 per day for failing to meet water quality standards or implementation schedules, and authority for the secretary of the interior to seek immediate injunctive relief in emergency situations (including water pollution hazards or irreversible damage to water quality).

4. Cleaning Up Federal Facilities. A task force idea that Nixon strongly endorsed was the issuing of an executive order requiring that all federal facilities conform to then-existing air and water quality standards. The order stated that all facilities had to comply by the end of 1972—and thus committed the federal government to a $359 million program to achieve this objective. The order also required that all federal facilities built in the future must be pollution-free and that funds must be included for air and water pollution control at time of construction. . . ."A must," the President wrote. "We can't ask industry and states and cities to act if we don't set an example."

5. Outdoor Recreation. The task force reported that only about 3 percent of federal lands and 25 percent of federal recreational areas were situated within convenient reach of large metropolitan areas; parks were simply not near where most people lived. Moreover, only middle and upper income groups could enjoy them: the "minimum entrance fee" was a family car and $200 in your pocket to get there and home again. As Nixon later said in his environmental message to Congress,

> Thousands of acres in the heart of metropolitan areas were reserved for only minimal use by Federal installations. . . . Until now the uses to which Federally-owned

properties were put has largely been determined by who got them first. As a result, countless properties with enormous potential as recreation areas linger in the hands of agencies that could just as well—or better—locate elsewhere. . . .

Converting federal property into urban parks, although a good way to bring parks closer to where people lived, was only a partial answer. Much more money to acquire lands and to develop recreational facilities was needed. The Land and Water Conservation Fund, established in 1964, was authorized annual appropriations of $200 million to buy lands for the National Park System and to establish a matching grant program for states and cities to acquire and develop their own parks, but in the Johnson years obligations to the fund had lagged far below authorizations. Nixon increased the Land and Water Conservation Fund from $200 to $300 million. Later he proposed establishment of the first urban national parks in New York and San Francisco harbors. But by 1976 even the $300 million annual funding level seemed inadequate to finance the growing need for urban parks.

Environmental Foresight

In retrospect, the proposals of the Nixon task force might seem modest. Strip mining, land use, control of pesticides and noise, and a tax to reduce sulfur dioxide, for example, had been either incompletely studied or not even thought of at the time of the President's message. Nor were any very useful cost-benefit studies of various pollution abatement scenarios available. That came later when Congress began to increase the environment budget and tighten pollution standards beyond what the President proposed. . . .

In spite of these shortcomings, it was a beginning and, in the author's opinion, a remarkable one. A set of conditions existed simultaneously that allowed the federal government to do something that it rarely does well—respond quickly to a problem. The President was interested and wanted to move, and so did Congress. A dedicated group of fine young people was able to work long hours to pull together a bewildering set of issues that were the responsibility of agencies scattered throughout the federal bureaucracy. The group produced a coherent set of recommendations that emerged as a comprehensive, thirty-seven-point program encompassing twenty-three separate pieces of legislation and fourteen administrative actions. Nixon could say without exaggeration on television and radio the day he sent his environmental message to Congress: "This is the most far-reaching and comprehensive message on conservation and restoration of natural resources ever submitted to Congress by a President of the United States."

Congress Rather than Nixon Should Be Credited for Environmental Action

Jerry Voorhis

As president, Nixon was more interested in supporting business than the environment. Although he tried to be aggressive on environmental issues, he was very concerned about the impacts such reforms might have on business. In addition, the president backed some programs that clearly harmed the environment. He ignored the expansion of clean hydroelectric power in favor of fossil fuels, backed the development of the supersonic airplane, and was very hesitant to place pollution controls on the automobile industry.

In this selection from his book on Nixon, philanthropist and educator Jerry Voorhis claims that Congress was responsible for most of the meaningful environmental legacies of Nixon's period in office, including the appropriation of sufficient funding and proposed restrictions on automobile exhaust. Voorhis served as a congressman from 1936 to 1946, when he was defeated by Richard Nixon.

THE ENVIRONMENT WAS NOT A MAJOR ISSUE IN THE CAMpaign for the presidency in 1968. But Dr. Barry Commoner [an environmental expert] and his associates at Washington University, St. Louis, were being listened to more and more as they warned of the dangers ahead unless the thrust of technology were reversed. Rachel Carson's book, *The Silent Spring*, once dismissed as extreme alarmist writing, was being taken seriously; and Senator [Edmund] Muskie was in demand as a speaker on environmental subjects. His address to the 1969 Consumer Assembly, titled "The Last Clear Chance," likened the present generation to a person who had the last clear chance to avoid a fatal accident. He plainly told his audience that the next very few decades would decide whether Earth would have a bright future or none at all as a home for human life.

By the year 1970, the second year of the Nixon presidency, Congress, the President, newspapers, magazines, television and radio were competing with one another for leadership in the fight against pollution.

So were an increasing number of popular organizations. Some of these, like the Sierra Club, cooperatives and organizations of consumers, had been at it for some time. Others were brand new associations, formed for the specific purpose of fighting one part or another of the battle.

Environmental organizations brought awareness to the public about the damage being wrought on the planet by large corporations and the lavish lifestyles of many Americans.

Much of the attack was levelled—quite properly—against corporations which had for decades been fouling the air and water with smoke and wastes. Governmental action was obviously called for. But increasingly it was realized that a basic culprit in the piece was the very high standard of living of the American people. Emphasis was on material satisfactions, comforts and luxuries. And these were demanding more and more power from the Earth.

How long the world's resources of fossil fuels would last at accelerating levels of consumption became an openly discussed question. So did the safety, or lack of it, of the much-promised power source from nuclear reactors. How long could the great American "love affair" with the automobile be allowed to continue? Was it not long past the time for a massive drive to develop the cheap, efficient mass transportation systems which workers so badly needed to get to jobs, and which the nation needed to replace half the automobile traffic? Was the craze for air conditioning an indulgence of the present generation which would be a major factor in robbing future generations of their rightful heritage? Were certain fertilizers and pesticides—DDT for example—the lethal danger to the environment which some scientists contended?

These and other questions were being asked. And answers demanded—especially by the young people who had most at stake.

Nixon Places Business Above the Environment

There were those who asked another question, this time a political one. Why was the Nixon Administration neglecting completely government development of the one time-tested method of producing power which did not pollute at all? This was—and is—hydro-electric power. Out of its deference to the private power monopoly, no doubt, the Administration was then, and continued throughout its course, refusing to inaugurate any significant hydro projects at all.

It was true that in his state of the union address of January 1970, Mr. Nixon had dramatically pledged himself to a $10 billion program of environmental clean-up, modestly labelling it "the most costly and comprehensive program in the field ever in history." Mr. Nixon declared: "I shall propose to this Congress a $10 billion nationwide clean-waters program to put modern municipal waste treatment plants in every place in America where they are needed, and get them built in five years." Only $4 billion of this was to be Federal money, the rest to come from the hard-pressed states. And his own Secretary of Interior, Walter Hickel, was joining Senator Muskie in saying that some three times the President's figure would be needed just to bring municipal water and sewer systems up to date.

The President did create a number of commissions, chief among them the Environmental Protection Agency. And before his first term was over he had recommended the spending of considerably more money on environmental programs than had ever been done by previous administrations.

But his performance on the practical front of action against polluters and pollution was, in general, a different story.

Congress Did More for the Environment than Nixon

Congress was way ahead of him. In 1969 it had passed the National Environmental Policy act, authored by Democratic Senator Henry Jackson of Washington. And in part to provide staff for the Council of Environmental Affairs, created by the Jackson bill, Senator Muskie had authored the Water Quality Improvement Act of 1969. Strangely, Mr. Nixon had supported the Jackson bill but declared that the Muskie bill "would be a mistake."

In 1970 President Nixon requested just $214 million for water and sewer grants to cities and towns, whereas Congress appropriated $800 million. In August, 1970, Mr. Nixon actually vetoed the HUD [Housing and Urban Development] appropriation bill because, he contended, it contained $350 million "too much" for water and sewer grants. And he kept some $200 million of funds actually appropriated by Congress for this purpose impounded in the Office of Management and Budget.

In June 1970 other events transpired which it seemed hard to reconcile with the high-level oratory of Mr. Nixon's state of the union message of six months before. Newspapers reported on June 7 that actual work on anti-pollution projects had been sharply reduced because of an order from the Administration to cut expenditures. Jacob Dumelle, head of the Federal Water Quality Administration for the Lake Michigan region, called the order "unfortunate" and said it "jeopardizes vital summer programs." At the time there were only 2,200 people employed in the Federal anti–water pollution program compared to 1,500,000 *civilian* employees in the Defense Department.

At this same time—the summer of 1970—President Nixon was demanding that Congress appropriate $290 million as first installment on development of a supersonic air transport plane, the total cost of which was estimated to be $4 billion. This money was to be a virtual gift of taxpayers' money to a private manufacturer. Furthermore from the standpoint of environmental pollution, it was, to say the least, undesirable. Environmental scientists feared that such planes would upset natural meteorological balance in the upper atmosphere where they would fly, and thus expose the Earth's surface to excessive radiation. No one even attempted to deny that the plane would subject Earth, its people and its other living things, to a bombardment of sonic booms. Its only conceivable use would be to get a handful of rich travellers to Paris in a couple of hours' less time. The President's ad hoc task force on the project, the Federal Council on Environmental Quality, and the President's Science Advisory Committee had all recommended against the SST. And a number of state legislatures had passed laws forbidding such planes to land on their soil.

Nonetheless the Administration persisted. Mr. Nixon

made this a major personal recommendation to the Congress.

But Congress refused to obey in the 1970 session.

A year later the project was pushed again by the President. And again after long and bitter debate, the Congress refused to authorize it. Whereupon Mr. Nixon declared he would find some other way to get a supersonic air transport built in the United States. There the matter rests.

In December, 1970, House and Senate conferees agreed on the final form of the Muskie bill to require automobile manufacturers to produce a nearly pollution-free automobile by 1975. The bill did empower the Administrator of the Environmental Protection Agency, which President Nixon had established, to grant a one-year extension, to 1976, if it was persuaded, by evidence, that this was necessary. The bill contained another important provision. It required the Administrator of the EPA to take into account not only the technology developed by the petitioning automobile company but also any better technology developed by independent engineering concerns.

The Nixon Administration joined the automobile companies in opposing the Muskie legislation. The Secretary of Health, Education, and Welfare wrote to the Senate committee considering the bill urging that a later deadline than 1975 or 1976 be put into the bill.

As well he might have done. For the Administration's own bill in the same field merely set 1980 as a "goal" for achievement of nearly pollution-free cars and contained no requirement whatever that the goal be met!

It was becoming less and less difficult to tell whether the real defenders of planet Earth were in the Congress or the White House.

Nixon's Environmental Policies Reflected the Will of the American People

Tom Wicker

Many have claimed that Richard Nixon was a politician who, instead of taking strong stands on issues, moved with the political tide. By the late 1960s, for example, concern about pollution had grown widespread. Such concern was clear even among the "Silent Majority," as Nixon called his many supporters, and Nixon felt he had to respond.

New York Times columnist Tom Wicker, in the following excerpt from his book *One of Us: Richard Nixon and the American Dream,* contends that Nixon's environmental measures were responses to this public demand for action. While Nixon himself was clearly pro-business rather than pro-environment, Wicker points out, he had the responsibility as America's highest elected official to address growing concerns about environmental quality.

RICHARD NIXON WAS NO MORE AN ENVIRONMENTAL THAN a racial activist when he entered the White House; he had only a dim view of the environment as a political issue and delegated the subject largely to [his main advisor on domestic issues, John] Ehrlichman. Again, however, he found that he had little choice but to address an unavoidable issue.

Excerpted from *One of Us: Richard Nixon and the American Dream*, by Tom Wicker. Copyright ©1991 by Tom Wicker. Reprinted by permission of Random House, Inc.

The imperative was not court decisions but public opinion—an "environmental revolution," as it was termed by John Whitaker, one of Nixon's primary environmental aides, later undersecretary of the interior, in remarks at the Hofstra conference [on Nixon's domestic record] in 1987. This was not a resurgence of the old Teddy Roosevelt–style concern for "conservation" of natural resources in great national parks. It was instead a growing demand that the *quality* of the environment be improved and protected everywhere—that stream water should be clean, forests and species protected, natural beauty preserved, and the air over American cities less polluted.

The *need* for such a movement dated far back into early industrial America but an important modern starting point would be Detroit's profit-driven decision in the early post–World War II years to build bigger cars with bigger engines—cars emitting, therefore, more carbon monoxide and other pollutants. Before long, "smog" became a new word in the American lexicon, and—worse—a choking new cloud over American life.

The first, and perhaps the strongest, catalyzing force of the modern environmental movement was the publication of *Silent Spring* by Rachel Carson in 1963, with its dramatic and moving disclosures of the effects of DDT and other pesticides on plants, animals and earth. In direct response to the newly exposed threat of DDT, for example, the Environmental Defense Fund, still a major force in national politics, was born on Long Island.

Other seminal events followed *Silent Spring*—the fight against Consolidated Edison's plan to put a power plant atop Storm King Mountain along the Hudson River, national revulsion against a proposal (endorsed by that great outdoorsman, Barry Goldwater) to build power dams in the Grand Canyon, most of all perhaps the oil spill in the Santa Barbara Channel off California in 1969. As early as Lyndon Johnson's "Great Society" speech in 1964, he had declared:

Our parks are overcrowded, our seashores overburdened. Green fields and dense forests are disappearing. . . . [O]nce our natural splendor is destroyed, it can never be recaptured.

Some substantial legislation was passed in the Johnson years, mainly under the leadership of Senator Edmund Muskie of Maine. Notably, a start was made on controlling smog and preventing water pollution; after a hard fight, and with substantial support from Mrs. Johnson, a highway beautification bill also became law.

Earth Day and Politics

In the 1968 campaign, however, neither Nixon nor Hubert Humphrey—both men of sensitive political antennae—spoke more than cursorily of environmental concerns, despite Muskie's presence on the Humphrey ticket. Obviously, the candidates felt no need to. Nor were they pressed to speak on the subject by the reporters trailing them.

In 1969, after Nixon told him of a White House meeting with groups including the Sierra Club, Henry Kissinger asked: "What *is* the Sierra Club?" Kissinger's ignorance was not atypical at the time. In April 1970, however, public opinion took a mighty surge forward with the unprecedented success of Earth Day.

The passage of twenty years may have obscured the impact of that event: ten thousand schools, two thousand colleges and universities, nearly every community in the nation, took part. Huge crowds turned out for environmental observances—for example, one hundred thousand in New York City for an "eco-fair" in Union Square. Congress adjourned to permit its members to attend teach-ins on the environment. All three television networks featured Earth Day events and the Public Broadcasting System turned over all its daytime programs to the subject.

Immense national interest was now visible. The envi-

Nixon Pledges to Fight Air Pollution

In a presidential press conference held July 30, 1970, Nixon pointed out that air pollution was a problem for all leaders, not just New York City mayor John Lindsay.

Q: Mr. President, do you have any magical powers that you may invoke to help the people on the east coast breathe a little easier, or do you consider that Mayor Lindsay's problem?

The President: I think Mayor Lindsay has enough problems without wishing that one on him. The problem on the east coast, of course, reminds all of us who are southern Californians that with all of the kidding we have been taking about our smog, it isn't limited to us.

I also would remind the people on the east coast and in California that it isn't limited to the United States. It's a problem in Tokyo, it's a problem in Rome, it's a problem in all of the great industrial areas of the world now.

There isn't any short-range answer. We can't get the kind of automobile engine which will be pollution-free in a year or 2 years or 3 years. But there are certain things that can be done now. . . .

I would only say this, that it was perhaps fortunate in a way that the east coast saw this problem in such a massive manner. Now we realize that we don't have much time left and it is time for the Congress to get the environmental message and all of the recommendations that I have made in February—a very strong message and very strong measures—to get them on the front burner and act on them now, because this is an area where we cannot wait.

The Nixon Presidential Press Conferences, Earl M. Coleman Enterprises, 1978.

ronment suddenly rose high on the national agenda; and newly formed groups like the National Resources Defense Council could channel that interest into effective pressures on Congress, the executive, the states.

In May 1969, a private White House poll had found only 1 percent of respondents who believed the environment was the most important issue facing the new president. Two years later, as John Whitaker recalled it, another survey found that the figure had increased to 25 percent of respondents; and in the second poll, the environment was surpassed as an issue of concern only by Americans' personal economic worries. . . .

After the Earth Day demonstrations, Richard Nixon, pragmatic as always, moved not to flee or thwart but to seize upon that environmental consensus—another instance suggesting that purity of motive is not the only, or necessarily the best, impulse from which a political leader can act usefully. Sometimes, he or she will be more effective when driven by political forces, when scrambling to get out in front of supposed "followers." . . .

Does Environmentalism Pay?

Cost-benefit ratios were a real concern to [Nixon], so much so that the environmentalist-scientist Barry Commoner pointed out at Hofstra that it produced what he considered one of the worst flaws in Nixon's environmental record, the imposition of the Office of Management and Budget's authority over the decisions of the EPA [Environmental Protection Agency]. Bringing cost-benefit analysis to environmental questions meant that unless the economic benefits outstripped the costs of an environmentally sound action, it should not be taken.

Commoner charged that Nixon the politician, sensitive to the public response to Earth Day, had merely "latched on to a motherhood issue" in 1970; and that so far from leading the environmental movement in a positive way, he had proceeded to weaken congressional efforts to write effective laws. Richard Nixon "began the process of . . . putting loopholes into the law," Commoner asserted. One result, he said, was that clean air legislation had removed only 14 percent of pollutants, though it had been theoretically designed to achieve a 90 percent reduction.

Commoner cited a Nixon appearance before the Economic Club of Detroit on September 23, 1971, less than two years after his ringing State of the Union message on protection of the environment. The president had shown his true colors, Commoner said, before an audience that included many automobile executives—and Nixon certainly did stress, in answer to a question, his cost-benefit concerns:

> It is vitally important . . . that more attention must be given to the cost factor as well as to the factor that we are all interested in—of cleaning up our air and cleaning up our water. . . .
>
> [W]hen the Congress, or an administration carrying out the will of the Congress, sets certain standards . . . we must weigh against that: How many jobs is it going to cost? And, if it is going to cost a disproportionate number of jobs . . . then we have to reevaluate the decision. . . .
>
> We are committed to cleaning up the air and cleaning up the water. But we are also committed to a strong economy, and we are not going to allow the environmental issue to be used sometimes falsely and sometimes in a demagogic way basically to destroy the system—the industrial system that made this the great country that it is.

Into these remarks undeniably pleasing to business ears must be factored the occasion: no president was likely to tell the Economic Club of Detroit—or anyone else for that matter—that jobs and the economy were of little concern to him; nor should he. Nixon's criticism, moreover, was not of the environmental issue itself but of its false or demagogic use (though he cited no examples).

Besides, cost-benefit analysis cannot be wholly disregarded even in environmental matters. To use an example Whitaker cited, suppose spending one hundred dollars to clean up 95 percent of an environmental problem would be justified; would it be equally justified to spend another hundred dollars to get at the remaining 5 percent? Perhaps; but surely *the question* is reasonable. . . .

Barry Commoner, a man of outspoken views and formidable knowledge, had a point of view to push, anyway; he stated the candid belief that profit-driven corporate decisions (like Detroit's deliberate post–World War II policy to build bigger cars) were at the root of all environmental problems. In that view, regulatory legislation after the fact, like that signed by Nixon, could never do the job; the only effective way to protect the environment was to give the public a voice in corporate decisions. That was not a procedure likely to be furthered by a president who had pledged, in Commoner's view, not to destroy the free market system. But what president ever did want to destroy it?

Commoner was nevertheless on target concerning Nixon's basic views. Ehrlichman has testified to the president's lack of fundamental personal interest in the environment, and Whitaker conceded that Nixon was "a very strong capitalist" who had the "visceral, gut reaction we have to be careful about how fast we go in being Mister Clean." And to a speech writer, Nixon once remarked, "In a flat choice between smoke and jobs, we're for jobs.". . .

Nixon Was Uninterested in Environmentalism

Nixon the politician undoubtedly did seize upon the environment as "a motherhood issue," while Nixon the capitalist (Garry Wills's classic liberal, the self-made man) harbored reservations about the cost to business and the possible loss of jobs (a preoccupation with him). Nor would he have been the first president (both Roosevelts and Wilson come to mind) who pushed or accepted useful but limited social legislation in order to preempt more radical measures.

In all likelihood, too, the "group of people" who pushed environmentalism and consumerism did not appeal to a president who valued hard-nosed realism—which, to him, would have been represented by the [Lee] Iacoccas of the world, men determined to keep profits up by holding the price of cars down, with as little concession as possible to safety and environmental considerations.

Besides, Nixon's real interest lay in other matters. "A visit to a sewage treatment plant in suburban Chicago (to show support for a Clean Water Act) somehow didn't make Richard Nixon feel like the leader of the Free World," Ehrlichman observed. "But the point is that President Nixon *did* visit sewage plants and energy generators. . . ."

Does Nixon's personal attitude matter all that much, in light of the results? How much difference is there between an achievement of personal conviction and one of political necessity? If, sometimes, the former might be more sweeping, the latter certainly occurs more often; and as the perfect can be the enemy of the good, too high an aim can sometimes miss altogether.

On the environment, as in school desegregation, Nixon was pragmatist, as well as opportunist. He recognized that he had little choice in the face of the "environmental revolution" but to act; the force of public opinion was too great to resist, as had been the force of court desegregation orders. Presidents are elected to make such judgments, and devise acceptable means of doing the necessary.

Nixon the Centrist

Nixon the centrist again chose a middle course—for example, in proposing a permissible level of auto emissions higher than that put forward by Detroit but lower than that approved by a "credit card" Congress (as he sometimes termed it) not then much constrained by budgetary worries. If he established the EPA, he also gave the Office of Management and Budget significant power over it; if he signed environmental legislation, he tried to limit the spending Congress was willing to approve; if he failed to please Barry Commoner, he also displeased the auto industry—the latter unquestionably of more concern to him. It's hard to suppose that another president would or could have passed up the opportunity the environmental revolution laid before Nixon. It's equally hard to believe, in light of the inherent opposition to that revolution, that someone else in the Oval Office would or could have gone much farther than Nixon did in meeting public demand for action. In fact, no president since *has* gone farther, though Jimmy Carter should be given credit for trying. Richard Nixon, moreover, can hardly be imagined ducking for eight years the acid rain issue, as Ronald Reagan did.

Ehrlichman, a far more enthusiastic environmentalist than his boss, ranks Nixon's response to the environmental revolution second only to school desegregation as the major domestic achievement of his administration. And he believes that no matter what the president's original reservations, Nixon wound up being "rather proud" of his environmental record.

TRYING TO
END THE
VIETNAM WAR

Nixon Secretly Expanded U.S. Involvement in Vietnam

Joan Hoff

By the late 1960s, the Vietnam War, begun and expanded by
Nixon's predecessors Kennedy and Johnson, seemed to be drag-
ging on and on. A growing number of Americans demanded
that the U.S. soldiers stationed in Vietnam be brought home,
and Nixon won the 1968 presidential election in part because of
his promise to get the United States out of the conflict. Although
Nixon did begin troop withdrawals soon after his inauguration,
he also authorized actions that expanded the war, namely the secret bombing of Cambodia in the spring of 1969. Critics
charged not only that Nixon had broken his campaign promises, but also that his covert actions had been illegal, since Cambodia was not an official combatant.

As Indiana University professor of history Joan Hoff points
out in this selection from her book, *Nixon Reconsidered*, the
president had no clear plan for ending the conflict in Vietnam.
Instead, he expanded the war but also had his main foreign policy adviser, Henry Kissinger, engage in secret negotiations to
end it. The secret bombing of Cambodia was intended to pressure the North Vietnamese to continue negotiations while
Nixon kept up the appearance of pulling U.S. forces out of Vietnam. This strategy, Hoff suggests, left Vietnam in worse shape
than before.

I T WAS CLEARLY IN NIXON'S PSYCHIC AND POLITICAL SELF-interest to end the war in Vietnam as soon as possible. "It is essential that we end this war, and end it quickly," he said while campaigning for his party's nomination in 1968, only to add the fateful words: "But it is essential that we end it in such a way that we can win the peace." Although Nixon came to office committed to negotiating a quick settlement to a massive undeclared war that his administration had inherited from Kennedy and Johnson, he ended up expanding and prolonging the conflict in the name of peace and honor.

In the process, he could never build the domestic consensus he needed to continue the escalated air and ground war (even with dramatically reduced U.S. troop involvement) and to ensure passage of some of his domestic programs. For Nixon (and Kissinger), Vietnam became a symbol of influence in the Third World, which, in turn, was but one part of their geopolitical or grand-design approach to international relations. The war in Southeast Asia had to be settled as soon as possible so as not to endanger other elements of Nixonian diplomacy and domestic policy.

According to his book *No More Vietnams* (1985), Nixon viewed that conflict as military, moral, and multinational in scope. Consequently, he first sought to bring military pressure to bear on the North Vietnamese in order to speed up the negotiating process. There is little indication, however, that this approach succeeded. The Communist Vietcong forces correctly counted on opposition in the United States to the announced bombing and invasion of Cambodia in April 1970 and of Laos in February 1971. Likewise, Nixon's commitment to the war as a "moral cause" did not ring true, as the carnage in that civil war increased despite American troop withdrawals. Finally, the president never succeeded in convincing the country that quick withdrawal from Vietnam would "damage American strategic interests" all over the world. So ending the draft and bringing the troops home did not end Congress's opposition to the Vietnam War (although these actions did diminish the size of antiwar demonstrations beginning in 1971) because Nixon had failed to convince that branch of government (and many Americans) that the conflict in this tiny Third World country warranted the military, moral, and multinational importance he attributed to it. Neither he nor Kissinger has ever admitted that their policies destabilized most of Indochina and led to horrific events in Cambodia, Laos, and Vietnam in which hundreds of thousands of people lost their lives.

Instead, Nixon allowed Kissinger as special assistant to the president for national security affairs to become egocentrically involved in secret negotiations with the North Vietnamese from August 4, 1969, to January 25, 1972 (when they were made public, over Kissinger's protestations). As a result, only marginally better terms were reached in 1973 than had been agreed to in 1969. The significance of the 1972 agreement by Hanoi (capital of North Vietnam) that President Nguyen Van Thieu, the president of South Vietnam, could remain in power in return for allowing its troops to remain in South Korea palls when compared to the additional 20,552 American lives lost during this three-year period. Moreover, by 1973, despite or because of Vietnamization, the government in Saigon (capital of South Vietnam) was inherently weaker than it had been in 1969. The most embarrassing evidence of this weakness occurred when President Ford was forced to order an emergency evacuation of the last remaining U.S. troops from Saigon in April 1975.

On the tenth anniversary of the peace accords ending the war in Vietnam, Nixon admitted to me that "Kissinger believed more in the power of negotiation than I did." He also said that he "would not have temporized as long" with the negotiating process had he not been "needlessly" concerned with what the Soviets and Chinese might think if the United States pulled out of Vietnam precipitately.

A more likely scenario is that Nixon had no clear idea

in 1969 of how to end the war quickly. His immediate options seemed to be the initiation of secret negotiations with the North Vietnamese and/or the resumption of overt, massive bombing attacks over North Vietnam. At the same time he was probably more worried about the reaction of the general public or antiwar movement to a renewal of the bombing of North Vietnam than about that of the People's Republic of China or the Soviet Union. Both countries had, after all, tolerated Johnson's bombings of North Vietnam. So he chose to pursue secret negotiations *and* secret expansion of the war into Cambodia and Laos, thus destabilizing all of Indochina, not simply Vietnam. As a result there was neither peace nor honor in Vietnam by the time the war was finally concluded on January 27, 1973. Another plausible, but not entirely convincing, argument can be made, in retrospect at least, that Nixon's (and Kissinger's) initial concern about public relations—more than concern about diplomatic relations with China and the USSR—locked them into the same compromise on military strategy that Johnson had pursued, ultimately prolonging the war and resulting in unintended negative consequences for all of Indochina.

Widening the War Covertly

Under President Johnson, the Joint Chiefs of Staff [JCS] had repeatedly requested permission to bomb Communist sanctuaries in Cambodia. The last of the requests was to the outgoing Democratic administration on December 13, 1968, when the JCS asked for "standby authority . . . to pursue North Vietnam Army Viet Cong (NVAVC) Forces into Cambodia following major enemy offensives mounted and supported from Cambodia." They reiterated this position to the incoming Republican administration when Nixon, on January 21, 1969, asked [Chief of Staff of the Army] General Wheeler in [National Security Study Memorandum] NSSM 1 to provide a "study of the feasibility and utility of quarantining Cambodia against the receipt of supplies and equipment for support of Viet Cong and North Vietnamese Army."

Refusing to Accept Defeat

In a 1970 address, Nixon defended his decision to continue U.S. involvement in Vietnam:

Whether I may be a one-term President is insignificant compared to whether by our failure to act in this crisis the United States proves itself to be unworthy to lead the forces of freedom in this critical period in world history. I would rather be a one-term President and do what I believe is right than to be a two-term President at the cost of seeing America become a second-rate power and to see this Nation accept the first defeat in its proud 190-year history.

Richard M. Nixon, national address, April 30, 1970.

Early in 1969, in response to this memo, the JCS recommended "military actions which might be applied in concert or incrementally, subject to their political acceptability." In light of such proposed Nixonian innovations as renewal of the Paris peace talks, troop withdrawals, and Vietnamization, this request may have seemed a more reasonable way to ensure an orderly replacement of American units with forces from the Army of the Republic of Vietnam than it had during the last months of the Johnson administration.

President Johnson had refused to consider a mutual, let alone unilateral, withdrawal of troops. On December 21, 1968, his secretary of defense, Clark M. Clifford, had requested from the JCS a reassessment of the situation in Cambodia in relation to the air and naval bombardment of

North Vietnam, and said that the reply "would provide a basis for review of military operations in Cambodia and their possible relation to the broader question of US diplomatic objectives in Southeast Asia." In an analysis of the JCS response, Secretary [of Defense] Laird was told that in view of the "political ramifications" of the recommendations, the National Security Council would have to consider these proposals. Given Clifford's reason for this reassessment, Johnson administration officials perhaps might have been more inclined toward the bombing of Cambodia than was the president. At least this is how the JCS chose to interpret Clifford's memorandum for Nixon's secretary of defense, Melvin Laird.

Nixon's attitude did prove quite different from Johnson's. On January 8, 1969, while still president-elect, Nixon informed Kissinger in a note that he wanted "a precise report on what the enemy has in Cambodia and what, if anything, we are doing to destroy the buildup there." He concluded these early thoughts on the matter of bombing Cambodia with the words: "I think a very definite change of policy toward Cambodia probably should be one of the first orders of business when we get in." Later that month, top military officials had to face the unhappy prospect of significant troop withdrawals. General Wheeler indicated at the January 25 NSC [National Security Council] meeting that the military was doing everything it could in Vietnam except bombing the Cambodian sanctuaries, but he added that "a small reduction of US forces . . . would help Nixon domestically and convey the image of a self-confident South Vietnam." Subsequently he wrote to General Creighton Abrams, Commander, United States Military Assistance Command, Vietnam (COMUSMACV), that on the basis of this meeting and later conversations with Secretary Laird, troop reductions were imminent. "At the present time," Wheeler told Abrams, "public discussion of withdrawals or troop reduction in Vietnam should be limited to mutual withdrawal within the context of the Paris negotiations. I myself propose to keep silent." Wheeler strongly urged Abrams to "quietly put the damper on any public discussion [of troop withdrawals] by senior U.S. officers," and to request this same silence from General Cao Van Vien, President Thieu's chief of staff, and from other top South Vietnamese officials.

By February 6 President Thieu had publicly agreed to a "sizable" reduction in American troops. By March 28 (ten days after the first bombs were secretly dropped on Cambodian sanctuaries) the NSC used (with Abrams in attendance) Laird's term *Vietnamization* to describe the "de-Americanization" of the war based on significant troop withdrawals. On April 10 departments and agencies began planning schedules for Vietnamizing the war, and in June the first of many U.S. troop reductions was publicly announced by Nixon from Midway Island after a crucially important meeting in which he obtained (once again) Thieu's reluctant support for the beginning of these cutbacks of American military personnel.

Nixon faced public as well as military skepticism about the policy of Vietnamization being nothing more than a sophisticated form of appeasement. "Mr. President," wrote one disgruntled resident of Salt Lake City, "your current trip to Midway and your press releases has [*sic*] finally ended your political career as president. . . . If you are afraid to end the war that the United States has a superiority in you are selling the American people down the river of false hopes. . . . How can you possible [*sic*] live with the fact that a release of 25,000 Americans from Vietnam is a contribution to anything bewilders me."

The Decision to Bomb Cambodia Rather than North Vietnam

At the beginning of the Nixon administration, Secretary of Defense Laird (and, to a lesser degree, Secretary of State

Rogers) adamantly opposed the bombing of both North Vietnam and Cambodia because it would not be popular in Congress, the country, or the UN, let alone the attacked countries. In the first weeks of March, however, Laird endorsed the bombing of Cambodian sanctuaries as a better alternative to bombing North Vietnam—an option initially under consideration by the Nixon administration—even after the NVAVC increased attacks in February against major South Vietnamese cities. Cambodia, in other words, became a surrogate for the more drastic option of bombing North Vietnam.

At no time, however, did Laird believe that the bombing of Cambodia should be kept a secret. Much to the disdain of Ehrlichman and others close to Nixon, Laird seemed too much the politician on most issues and particularly on this one, because he was convinced that the United States had to pull out of Vietnam before losing any more domestic support. Curiously, Nixon's closest aides attributed even Laird's moderately consistent position on getting out of the war through Vietnamization purely to what Ehrlichman pejoratively called "constituency politics"—meaning that Laird was excessively beholden to Congress and the Pentagon. In fact, the greatest weakness of Laird's position was not his personal concern about congressional or military opinion but the fact that his Vietnamization program would take more time to implement than Nixon could spare, considering how public opinion stood on the war by the time he assumed office. Laird may have been excessively concerned about Congress and the Pentagon, but the president had much broader constituencies to satisfy. . . .

Nixon probably made his two initial decisions in February and March to bomb Cambodian sanctuary areas where, according to General Creighton W. Abrams's data, the least number of civilians were located. The president apparently retracted these decisions twice, not finally implementing his third decision until the middle of March.

Nixon's resolve was reinforced (as, indeed, it evidently needed to be) by the reported increase in North Vietnamese attacks in the intervening weeks on South Vietnamese cities. Nixon became increasingly impatient with top-secret military reports (and newspaper accounts) that continually noted "extensive evidence of enemy plans and preparations for large scale offensive operations [into South Vietnam]," telling Kissinger that he thought the United States and not the Communists should take the initiative.

U.S. troops search for Viet Cong forces. Despite promises of withdrawal, Richard Nixon actually expanded U.S. operations in Vietnam.

While Nixon formally authorized the secret bombing of Cambodia as a result of the March 18, 1969, NSC review, the command decision had actually been issued on March 16 and, according to Kissinger, the president had made his decision on March 15. The secret B-52 sorties over Cambodia lasted from March 18 to May 26 under the general code name MENU, with exact target areas given the unsavory titles of BREAKFAST, LUNCH, DINNER, SUPPER, DESSERT, and SNACK. A secret dual-bookkeeping system was used to report on the covert bombing of Cambodia until February 17, 1971. According to a September 1970 Department of Defense "White Paper," the purpose of MENU "was to protect American lives during the preparation for and actual withdrawal of U.S. military personnel from Southeast Asia by pre-empting imminent enemy offensive actions from the Cambodian sanctuaries into South Vietnam and against U.S. servicemen and women." But this does not explain why it was conducted in secret.

Some have attributed the secrecy of the bombings to Nixon's observation of Eisenhower privately threatening to use nuclear weapons if necessary to end the unpopular Korean War. This thesis is not very convincing, however, because there is no documented evidence that Nixon ever sent secret nuclear threats to either the North Vietnamese or the Chinese. Moreover, Eisenhower did not suppress information about the escalated bombings he ordered over North Korea in the spring of 1953. More convincing is the argument that fear of triggering new demonstrations and destroying the honeymoon period Nixon unexpectedly experienced until the fall of 1969 influenced the new administration's decision to cover up the initial bombing of Cambodia. Because Nixon's (and Kissinger's) concerns over public relations apparently prevented them from seriously pushing for the bombing of North Vietnam, they opted to bomb Cambodia and to keep it a secret.

Covering Up the Bombing of Cambodia

According to Kissinger's undocumented assertion, Nixon ordered Colonel Haig and an air force colonel, Ray B. Sitton, to meet with him on February 23 in Brussels, where he had flown to begin a tour of European nations. Gathering for this meeting on *Air Force One* (where the presidential accoutrements so impressed Kissinger that he meticulously described the push-button chairs and table in the middle of the only paragraph of his memoirs detailing the formulation of secret bombing plans) were Henry Kissinger, Alexander Haig, Ray Sitton, and H.R. Haldeman. Colonel Sitton had briefed administrative officials in January about bombing options in Vietnam. Haldeman, according to Kissinger's memoirs, was representing Nixon because the president's presence would have attracted too much attention. According to [investigative reporter] Seymour Hersh's account, however, Haldeman did not attend, leaving Nixon, who had called for the meeting, unrepresented. In this setting of three or four men (depending on whose story one accepts), the details of the bombing of a neutral, sovereign nation were worked out, although no independent documentation of this fact exists down to the present. All we have are a single paragraph in Kissinger's memoirs and Sitton's belated oral admission to Hersh that he, indeed, was the brains behind the double-bookkeeping system.

The inability of congressional committees or the Pentagon's own White Report team to identify or fix responsibility for devising and authorizing this system boggles the mind, since Sitton would have been a perfect scapegoat for everyone, including Nixon, during the Watergate investigations and impeachment inquiry of 1973–74. Yet Sitton's name never surfaced until he "readily described his activities" to Hersh, who contacted him on a tip from a "senior Pentagon official in mid-1979." Since the House Judiciary Committee considered, but voted down, the possibility of making the concealment of the bombing of Cambodia an article of impeachment against Nixon, it is all the more curious that Kissinger's and Haig's personal involvement in setting up the secret system has not discredited them for public office. At the time, of those who learned of the deceitful bookkeeping plan once the information was transmitted to Washington in February 1969, apparently only Laird cabled his reservations about it to Nixon.

General Wheeler's March 16 order authorizing a strike on COSVN [Central Office for South Vietnam] headquarters contained detailed information about answering press releases and questions about the bombings evasively. Similar instructions became standard for all orders directing secret flights over Cambodia throughout the spring of 1970. For example, almost a year after the strikes inside Cambodia began, a memorandum from General Wheeler authorizing certain targets contained standard wording for a news release, along with the following advice: "In the event press inquiries are received following the execution of these operations . . . U.S. spokesman will confirm that B-52s did strike on routine mission adjacent to the Cambodian border but state that he has no details and will look into this question. Should the press persist in its inquiries or in the event of a Cambodian protest concerning U.S. strikes in Cambodia, U.S. spokesman will neither confirm nor deny reports of attacks on Cambodia." Although the journalist Bill Beecher had reported the bombings on May 9, 1969, in the *New York Times,* the administration did not officially acknowledge this violation of Cambodia's sovereignty until the spring of 1972, and the public did not become fully aware of these covert strikes until a year later.

Individual or agency responsibility for the back-channel communications system that was employed to ensure optimum security of the MENU operation remains blurred. According to a Department of Defense "White Paper" issued on September 10, 1973, MENU flights ended in May 1970, but the dual-reporting system initially used in the field continued undetected for other covert strikes until February 1971, when duplicate information showed up on a downed aircraft operating under the code name FREEDOM DEAL outside designated target areas in Cambodia. This "error" resulted in the discontinuance of all such special reporting on subsequent special air (that is, covert) operations over Cambodia and Laos, proceeding under such code names as GOOD LUCK and PATIO. Since there were pro forma requests from the Cambodian government for U.S. air support between February 17, 1971, and August 15, 1973, sorties flown during this period became part of the official record. It was not until the summer of 1973, when the Senate Armed Services Committee opened hearings on the bombing of Cambodia, that the public first learned about the dual-reporting system used for covert land and air operations—a system for which no military or civilian official has yet taken responsibility.

Finally, on September 10, 1973, the Department of Defense issued its "Report on Selected Air and Ground Operations in Cambodia and Laos," which corrected all previous testimony and unclassified statistics presented to Congress by secretaries of defense Melvin Laird, Elliot Richardson, and James Schlesinger. Prior to this report, Congress had been systematically misled by top government officials, who presented false or misleading figures on the war's progress, never mentioning covert activity. A few members of Congress may have been informed by the Department of Defense about MENU and other covert military actions in Laos and Cambodia: Senators Richard Russell, John C. Stennis, and Everett Dirksen; Representatives Mendel Rivers, Leslie Arends, George H. Mahon; and the future vice president and president Gerald Ford.

A Failed Policy

To this day, however, no one has admitted that he personally ordered the falsification of figures or the double recordkeeping, which was allegedly devised by Sitton with the approval of Kissinger, Haig, and possibly Haldeman. "The necessity to minimize the likelihood of public speculation or disclosure was established within the NSC," according to the White Paper. "NSC guidance issued for the first MENU mission . . . remained representative of the guidance for all MENU missions. . . . The responsibility for development of detailed MENU procedures was delegated to the levels in DoD [Department of Defense] that normally controlled these procedures." No direct answer has ever been given as to how far up (or down) the civilian and military chains of command knowledge about Sitton's double-entry system went. . . .

Thus, a military policy cover-up—for which no one issued orders, which the NSC never explicitly discussed, but which Sitton now says he designed—presaged a domestic political cover-up.

In retrospect, the "illegal and criminally concealed" bombings and the subsequent overt invasion of Cambodia can be seen to have been multiply flawed policies. They did not bring psychological pressure to bear on negotiations, as hoped; they did not result in destruction of the COSVN headquarters; they needlessly angered a segment of the American population already suspicious of Nixon, and made Congress determined not to permit such unilateral, undemocratic exercise of executive authority in the future; they were initially inadequately funded through secretly diverted funds; and, finally, they never became major military objectives of the United States, but only a "short-term objective of ensuring the success of Vietnamization."

Consequently, the Joint Chiefs of Staff's initial jubilation over the civilian political decision to move into Cambodia waned quickly in the light of military reality. In a word, politics did not make for good military decisions, as General William W. Palmer's 1975 "End of Tour Report" documents in detail. The secret bombing of Cambodia failed, as did Nixon's general policy in Vietnam; but this particular policy failure should not be used to indict the entire NSC system. In other situations it performed adequately, and sometimes admirably, as in the EC-121 incident. The problem was that Nixon and Kissinger used it at their convenience rather than systematically.

Nixon Planned to End the War Through Vietnamization

Norman Podhoretz

The major reason why America entered the Vietnam War was that American leaders believed it was necessary to save South Vietnam, an independent nation, from falling under the control of the Communist regime in North Vietnam. Not only did many Americans believe that they needed to stop the spread of communism in general, they wanted to spare the South Vietnamese from the sufferings and restrictions of the North Vietnamese regime.

Norman Podhoretz, in this selection from his book *Why We Were in Vietnam*, claims that Richard Nixon was very concerned about preventing the North Vietnamese from taking over the South. But at the same time, Nixon wanted to reduce American involvement in the conflict. To accomplish both goals he developed a policy known as Vietnamization. This policy would, over time, turn full responsibility for the war over to the South Vietnamese government. Podhoretz is the author of several books and editor of the magazine *Commentary*.

N IXON *DID* INTEND TO LIQUIDATE THE AMERICAN COMBAT role in Vietnam. But not immediately or all at once. He even intended if possible to make peace. But not at the expense of turning South Vietnam over to the Communists. No one doubted that an *immediate* American withdrawal from Vietnam would mean just that, but those who expect-

Excerpted from *Why We Were in Vietnam*, by Norman Podhoretz (New York: Simon & Schuster, 1982). Copyright ©1982 by Norman Podhoretz. Reprinted by permission of the author.

ed it from Nixon thought that he would use his notorious cunning to disguise his acquiescence in a Communist victory—that he would, in other words, take the cosmetic or face-saving exit that Johnson had rejected before him. When they discovered that they were wrong, they accused Nixon of lying about getting out even when he began steadily reducing the number of American troops in Vietnam. . . .

Saving South Vietnam from Communism

Richard Nixon did not believe that the people of South Vietnam would be no worse off under Communism than they were under [South Vietnamese president Nguyen Van] Thieu. "I was aware that many Americans considered Thieu a petty and corrupt dictator unworthy of our support," he would write in his memoirs. "I was not personally attached to Thieu, but . . . the South Vietnamese needed a strong and stable government to carry on the fight against the efforts of the Vietcong terrorists, who were supported by the North Vietnamese army in their efforts to impose a Communist dictatorship on the 17 million people of South Vietnam."

Nor did Nixon have any doubt as to what such a dictatorship would mean to those 17 million South Vietnamese, "many of whom had worked for us and supported us": it would abandon them "to Communist atrocities and domination. When the Communists had taken over North Vietnam in 1954, 50,000 people had been murdered, and hundreds of thousands more died in labor camps. In 1968, during their brief control of Hué, they had shot or clubbed to death or buried alive more than 3,000 civilians whose only crime was to have supported the Saigon government." There would, then, be a bloodbath, followed by the institution of what Nixon's new National Security Adviser (and future Secretary of State), Henry Kissinger, called "the icy totalitarianism of North Vietnam."

But what was even more important to Nixon as President of the United States than the effect on South Vietnam of a Communist victory was its probable effect on the United States. "If we suddenly reneged on our earlier pledges of support, because they had become difficult or costly to carry out, or because they had become unpopular at home, we would not be worthy of the trust of other nations and we certainly would not receive it." He would act on "what my conscience, my experience, and my analysis told me was true about the need to keep our commitment. To abandon South Vietnam to the Communists now would cost us inestimably in our search for a stable, structured, and lasting peace."

In his ultimate objective, then, Nixon differed not in the slightest from Kennedy and Johnson; like them, he was determined to save South Vietnam from Communism. And like them too, he wanted to do it at the lowest possible cost. Kennedy had tried to do it with minimum involvement in the military operation in Vietnam; Johnson had tried to do it with minimum political disruption at home. Both had succeeded in the sense that South Vietnam had still not fallen to the Communists, but both had also failed to limit the cost. Johnson had been forced (as Kennedy would have been if he had lived) to pay a far higher price in military involvement than he had wished, and his effort to limit political disruption at home had resulted in more disruption than he had envisaged in his worst nightmares. Now it was Nixon's turn. . . .

Nixon Decides on the Policy of Vietnamization

When, in their meeting of October 1969, Nixon asked [British guerrilla warfare expert Sir Robert] Thompson "whether he thought it was important for us to see it through in Vietnam," Thompson replied, "Absolutely. In my opinion the future of Western civilization is at stake in the way you handle yourselves in Vietnam." Nixon also asked

Thompson what he thought of the idea of escalation. Thompson was against it "because it would risk a major American and worldwide furor and still not address the central problem of whether the South Vietnamese were sufficiently confident and prepared to defend themselves against a renewed Communist offensive some time in the future."

Listening to Nixon in Vietnam

John Paul Vann and Sir Robert Thompson, military advisers in Vietnam, were encouraged by a Nixon speech.

Vann escorted him [British guerrilla warfare expert Sir Robert Thompson] around the Delta for three days at the beginning of November. They were together to hear Nixon's watershed speech on Vietnam on November 3, 1969, listening to it over the radio in a district headquarters in Ba Xuyen Province, a former guerrilla bastion below the Bassac. Nixon had already ordered the withdrawal of 60,000 American troops to appease public opinion, and there was general expectation that he would use the occasion to announce a program for quick withdrawal of most of the rest and perhaps a cease-fire too. He instead appealed to "the great silent majority of my fellow Americans" for their patience and support while he prosecuted the war until he could obtain "peace with honor." The withdrawals would continue, but at a measured pace to permit the strengthening of the Saigon forces. Vann was elated by the speech, because it meant, he wrote a friend, that Nixon had decided "to tell the demonstrators to go to hell." Fortified by his days with Vann, Thompson reported back to Nixon that the Saigon side held a "winning position."

Neil Sheehan, *A Bright Shining Lie: John Paul Vann and America in Vietnam.* New York: Random House, 1988.

Nixon had already come to the same conclusion himself. Indeed, it was for this reason above all that he had decided on the strategy he would follow. His way of trying to save South Vietnam from Communism at minimum cost to the United States would be to turn the job over to the South Vietnamese themselves.

This idea was not, of course, invented by Nixon. Nor had it ever really been the intention of the United States to "Americanize" the war in Vietnam to the extent that had been done. "In the final analysis," Kennedy had said in September 1963, "it is their war. They are the ones who have to win or lose it." The following year, running against Goldwater, Johnson had made his by-now notorious promise that he would not send "American boys" to do the fighting that "Asian boys" had to do for themselves, and even as late as 1968, Johnson had said: "We and our allies can only help to provide a shield behind which the people of South Vietnam can survive and can grow and develop. On their efforts—on their determination and resourcefulness—the outcome will ultimately depend.". . .

It was only in response to Tet [a North Vietnamese offensive in January 1968] that serious plans began to be made to "de-Americanize" the war. A ceiling of 550,000 was placed on American troops, and a new emphasis was put on increasing the size and the quality of the South Vietnamese army. While still in office, Johnson said that he looked forward to a time when the American share of the responsibility for the security of South Vietnam would be greatly diminished, but not until Nixon became President did the process of disengagement actually get underway.

This process of "de-Americanization"—or "Vietnamization," as it came to be called instead at the insistence of Nixon's Secretary of Defense, Melvin Laird—began in June 1969 with the announcement that 25,000 American troops would soon be withdrawn and that additional withdrawals would follow at a rate to be determined by developments at the Paris peace talks, the level of enemy activity, and the progress of the South Vietnamese army. But as Nixon also stressed in a speech on November 3 of that year, which finally dashed all hope that he intended to withdraw immediately, the United States would (as he paraphrased the statement in his memoirs) "continue fighting until the Communists agreed to negotiate a fair and honorable peace or until the South Vietnamese were able to defend themselves on their own—whichever came first." Kissinger would put it more succinctly: "We were clearly on the way out of Vietnam by negotiation if possible, by unilateral withdrawal if necessary."

The Antiwar Movement Forced Nixon to Pull Back in Vietnam

Charles DeBenedetti
and Charles Chatfield

In 1970, Nixon decided to help South Vietnamese leader Nguyen Van Thieu in the invasion of Cambodia. Nixon's goal was to prevent the flow of supplies down the so-called Ho Chi Minh Trail, which connected North Vietnam with its sympathizers in the South but also ran partly through Cambodia. However, his expansion of the war into Cambodia inspired the largest protests yet against American involvement in the conflict.

In the following selection, University of Toledo history professor Charles DeBenedetti describes the wave of post-invasion protests, which eventually culminated in the shootings at Kent State University. He also notes how they spread beyond college campuses to include scientists, entertainers, and even Congress itself. In response to this widespread criticism of his policies, Nixon reduced his commitments in Cambodia and announced that he would reduce the number of ground troops in Vietnam.

Charles DeBenedetti is the main author of *An American Ordeal: The Antiwar Movement of the Vietnam Era*, from which the following article is excerpted. After his death in 1987, the book was finished by his colleague Charles Chatfield, a professor of history at Wittenberg University.

Excerpted from pages 278, 279, 280, 281, 284, and 285 of "Persisting in Withdrawal," chapter ten of *An American Ordeal: The Antiwar Movement of the Vietnam Era*, by Charles DeBenedetti (Syracuse, NY: Syracuse University Press, 1990). Reprinted by permission of the publisher.

NIXON INHERITED IN VIETNAM THE DILEMMA CREATED when Lyndon Johnson turned the corner in 1968, accepting a limited investment in war without foregoing the original goal of a viable, anticommunist regime in Saigon. That was the purpose of Vietnamization. The strategy changed—the United States was mobilizing Vietnamese resources and reducing its own forces—but the policy remained the same, a line of demarcation between North and South. Militarily, the challenge was to deny offensive capability to the North Vietnamese.

The Invasion of Cambodia

In March 1970 conservative Cambodian military elements led by General Lon Nol overthrew the neutralist regime of Prince Norodom Sihanouk. Military leaders of the Nixon and [South Vietnamese president Nguyen Van] Thieu governments seized the opportunity to deprive the North Vietnamese and Vietcong of their sanctuary and support base in Cambodia. U.S. planes and South Vietnamese artillery companies reinforced Cambodian army units attacking communist forces. Late in the month the Lon Nol government closed the port of Sihanoukville as a communist supply depot, and South Vietnamese forces opened their first major military engagement in Cambodia. A few days later, the communists launched an offensive of their own throughout South Vietnam. Saigon countered by attacking rest and supply sanctuaries in Cambodia until, in mid-April, its forces were streaming across the border where U.S. troops had taken up defensive holding positions. The Vietnam War had become more of an Indochina War.

Officially the United States government denied that it was involved in Saigon's decision to invade Cambodia. On 21 April the president made a special, nationally televised address, and he did not mention U.S. involvement in the operation. He simply announced that another 150,000

U.S. ground troops were scheduled to be withdrawn from South Vietnam (even though negotiations were stalled in Paris and the war seemed to be broadening).

The decline of organized antiwar opposition was illustrated by the fact that the initial, official expansion of the war into Cambodia was not seriously challenged. The lack of protest may have reflected popular willingness to allow the South Vietnamese to expand the conflict if that would help to strengthen the Saigon government.

The situation changed abruptly when, on April 30, President Nixon announced that he had ordered U.S. forces to join South Vietnamese troops in the invasion of Cambodia. This did not imply a widening of the war, the president insisted; rather, the attack was necessary to destroy the Cambodia-based command headquarters for enemy operations in South Vietnam, to disrupt enemy supply bases and lines, and thus to speed the pace of Vietnamization and U.S. troop withdrawals. Defending the invasion in personal and even apocalyptic terms, Nixon said that he would rather be a "one-term President" than accept "a peace of humiliation" which would result later in a larger war or surrender. "It is not our power but our will and character that is being tested tonight," he declared. "If, when the chips are down, the world's most powerful nation, the United States of America, acts like a pitiful, helpless giant, the forces of totalitarianism and anarchy will threaten free nations and free institutions throughout the world." As he spoke, U.S. and South Vietnamese troops advanced into southeastern Cambodia in Operation Ultimate Victory, the largest allied field operation in two years. They encountered light resistance, captured some 2,000 enemy troops, destroyed 8,000 bunkers, and took large supplies of weapons.

Whatever added time the Cambodian invasion may have bought for Vietnamization, it focused disaffection with the pace of withdrawal, aroused mistrust of the administration, and brought into the open the latent issue of executive authority to make war.

Antiwar Protests Erupt

Within minutes of the president's televised address, antiwar activists took to the streets in New York and Philadelphia, and protests erupted across the country in the following days. Scores of campuses from Maryland to Oregon rocked under a wave of marches and rallies marked by a sense of betrayal: the war was being expanded under the pretense of ending it. Critical reaction on Capitol Hill was swift and sharp, with warnings of "an impending constitutional crisis." Nixon had his back to the wall. During a meeting on 3 May, he coached aides to stand tough. Congressional supporters should be persuaded to accuse his detractors of "giving aid and comfort to the enemy," he said, emphasizing the point: "—use that phrase." Nixon continued, "Don't worry about divisiveness. Having drawn the sword, don't take it out—stick it in hard. . . . Hit 'em in the gut. No defensiveness." Kissinger later recalled that the commander in chief was "somewhat overwrought." Other aides thought he was on the verge of a nervous breakdown. . . .

[Protests] erupted spontaneously. A thousand University of Cincinnati students marched from the campus to a sit-in downtown, for instance, and large numbers of dissidents rallied at federal buildings in Nashville and Chicago. The great majority of protests were peaceful, although violence erupted at the University of Maryland and at Ohio University, and Stanford University students battled police in the worst rioting in the school's history. On 2 May, radical students attending a Black Panther support rally at Yale University appealed for a national student strike to demand an immediate U.S. withdrawal from Vietnam. The idea was endorsed by seven Ivy League student newspapers, in a joint editorial, as well as by the National Student Association, the SMC, and the New Mobe. Two days after the Yale meeting, Ohio national guardsmen fired into a milling crowd of students at Kent State University, killing four, wounding thirteen, and raising the American crisis to a new level of anguish.

The Kent State killings ignited anger which the White House only aggravated with the gratuitous comment that "when dissent turns to violence it invites tragedy." Within days, about 1.5 million students left classes, shutting down about a fifth of the nation's campuses for periods ranging from one day to the rest of the school year. Georgia state colleges suspended classes for two days; Governor Reagan closed the University of California system for five days; and Pennsylvania ordered its state universities to cease operations indefinitely. Forty-four percent of the country's colleges recorded peaceful protests, and 57 percent reported that the Cambodian invasion had made a "significant impact" on them. It was easily the most massive and shattering protest in the history of American higher education....

Angry over the invasion of Cambodia and fearful of domestic unrest, large numbers of liberals and elite dissidents attacked the administration and demanded antiwar action from Congress. Theodore Hesburgh of Notre Dame and Robert Goheen of Princeton were among thirty-seven presidents of major universities who urged Nixon to designate a terminal date for U.S. intervention. Two hundred fifty career officers in the State Department and the Foreign Service sent a joint letter of protest to Secretary of State William Rogers. Several leading Harvard University faculty members, including Thomas Schelling and Edwin Reischauer, met privately with their colleague Henry Kissinger to announce that they were breaking with administration policy, and several National Security Council staff members quit Kissinger's service in protest.

Historian Robert Beisner sensed movement without direction. "I don't think there's ever been a time since the founding of this nation—including even the days of Fort

Sumter," he told his students, "when the future direction of this country has been more problematical and unpredictable than right now." Normally apolitical groups, including Nobel science laureates, entertainment celebrities, musicians, architects, and publishers, were coalescing in opposition to the continuation of the war. Mostly they petitioned their government, but prominent local leaders in Oakland encouraged people to redeem and boycott U.S. savings bonds until the war ended.

Demonstrators organized sit-ins as one form of protest against the Vietnam War. Here, students form a sit-in at the Washington Monument in Washington, D.C.

Most important, dissidents turned to Congress, which, after the invasion of Cambodia, was inundated by the heaviest volume of telegrams on record. Overwhelmingly the messages were in opposition. Five days after Nixon announced the "incursion," the Senate Foreign Relations Committee accused him of usurping the legislature's warmaking power and denounced the "constitutionally unauthorized, Presidential war in Indochina." The charge, though quickly dismissed by the White House, began to take root. The president of the Amalgamated Clothing Workers Union demanded congressional constraints on the president. The American Civil Liberties Union abandoned its apolitical tradition to campaign for an immediate end of the war on the grounds that it was not constitutionally declared and therefore deprived Americans of their civil liberties. Several new groups formed to enjoin Congress to reassert its constitutional war-making powers. To this end, some faculty members at the University of Rochester launched a National Petition Committee of prominent intellectuals; 25 military officers on active duty formed a Concerned Officers Movement; 325 Asian experts and about 1,000 lawyers lobbied in Washington. Earl Warren, a former chief justice of the U.S. Supreme Court, told them that there was "no crisis within the memory of living Americans" comparable to the one enveloping the country. "The presidency is out of control," charged the *Christian Century*. The challenge for America became ever more widely perceived as "nothing less than the survival of constitutional democracy," and the antiwar movement, its orientation shifting now from the streets to congressional politics, embraced a national symbol which would become increasingly important in the following five years.

Nixon Backs Off

The Nixon administration was shocked by the breadth and anger of the outburst, especially after the killing of students; typically, it responded with ambivalence. For a while a siege atmosphere enveloped the White House. "We feared more demonstrations, more Kent States, an immobilized nation," one aide said. Kissinger recalled that "the fear of another round of demonstrations permeated all the thinking about Vietnam in the Executive Branch that summer— even that of Nixon, who pretended to be impervious." Although Agnew lashed out at critics as a "hard core of hell-raisers" and "charlatans of peace," the administration tried to blunt the force of antiwar discontent with reassurances. On 5 May, the president pledged that U.S. troops would not advance more than twenty-one miles into Cambodia without congressional approval. Three days later, Nixon promised that all American forces would be withdrawn from Cambodia by the end of June. Questioned about antiwar protesters, he declared that he agreed "with everything that they are trying to accomplish." Toward the end of the month, the administration announced that U.S. ground forces would be withdrawn from Cambodia within four weeks, but that U.S. air attacks would continue on an open-ended basis. By presidential fiat, America would participate in the new war in Cambodia, but in the least vulnerable way.

Nixon Dealt with the Antiwar Movement Effectively

Adam Garfinkle

In part because they faced being drafted into the conflict themselves, college students were the most visible of the many groups that actively protested the Vietnam War during Nixon's presidency. Protests on college campuses grew most widespread in 1970, when the president announced the expansion of the Vietnam conflict into neighboring Cambodia. These antiwar protests led to the shooting of students at Kent State and Jackson State Universities.

Adam Garfinkle, in the following selection from his book *Telltale Hearts: The Origins and Impact of the Vietnam Antiwar Movement*, claims that Nixon used public opinion effectively, even though he was held personally responsible for both the invasion of Cambodia and the university shootings. Antiwar protests declined drastically, Garfinkle notes, once Nixon adopted two strategies which addressed the immediate concerns of students: withdrawing American ground troops and ending the draft. Garfinkle is a resident scholar at the Foreign Policy Research Institute.

━━━━━

N IXON WAS CONSIDERED AN EXPERT IN FOREIGN POLICY, an interest he worked on and cultivated in his years out of public office. And a foreign affairs expert was precisely what many frustrated and disillusioned voters

Excerpted from *Telltale Hearts*, by Adam Garfinkle. Copyright ©1995 by Adam Garfinkle. Reprinted by permission of St. Martin's Press, LLC.

thought the country needed after watching the debacle in Vietnam develop. He was also considered anti-Communist enough to satisfy many Democrats who wondered whether irresolution in Vietnam indicated a softness in the overall U.S. position in the Cold War. The antiwar movement helped him too, as noted earlier, by adding to the backlash against the Democrats. If Norman Mailer hated Lyndon Johnson enough to think that there really was a "new Nixon," then perhaps others did too.

In one sense at least, there was a new Nixon—in domestic policy. But Nixon's vaunted secret plan to end the Vietnam War, which arguably was the factor that boosted him to victory over Hubert Humphrey in 1968 in a very close election, was never anything more than a de-emphasis on land action and an added emphasis on air power and negotiation from strength—a combination that U.S. military policy and diplomacy had already hit upon in the latter half of 1968. Nixon just packaged it for politics.

There was another sense in which Nixon was not new. He had a keen sense of his enemies—he even listed them, after all—and the radical antiwar movement was made up of the kinds of people Nixon hated most: the children of liberal establishment elitists, wealthy Jews, and violence-preaching blacks. If that hatred was not fairly clear at the time—and it really was—it has become clear since. At the president's behest, in ways both legal and illegal, the administration went after antiwar radicals with a vengeance. Compared to the principals of the Johnson administration, those in the Nixon administration thought about their opposition—of all sorts—in a more concentrated way.

This had everything to do with the personality of Richard Nixon, not any increased effectiveness on the part of the antiwar movement. Similarly, the kinds of attitudes that motivated the Watergate break-in owed little to Democratic prospects in 1972 and everything to the personality of the administration, formed from the very top.

Unlike the Democrats, who ultimately managed to use Watergate and subsequent related sins to unseat Nixon, the antiwar movement helped the new president out quite a lot in the early months of the administration. Even as the movement as a whole was gravitating back toward the center, the extremely photogenic activities of the hyperradical Left made it seem otherwise. Just as there are certain people who love the excitement and danger of storms, so Richard Nixon was a man who thrived on adversity. Thanks to the Black Panthers, the Weather Underground, and Rennie Davis's May Day Tribes [all protest groups], Richard Nixon could truly relish the storm. . . .

Protests Against Nixon and the Vietnam War

The invasion of Cambodia and the shootings at the Kent State and Jackson State universities in early May 1970 shut down college campuses across the United States in greater numbers than ever before. The reason had to do with the dramatic nature of events overseas: a pre-planned U.S. invasion of "yet another" country coming suddenly, and seemingly contradicting the de-escalatory tendencies of the Nixon administration. Another major part of the reason, clearly, was the deaths of university students; it was only *after* Kent State that the May 1970 demonstrations took on their vast scale. . . .

The important thing about the 1970 demonstrations is that they really were spontaneous outbursts. A 1970 Harris poll indicated demonstrations on 80 percent of American college campuses, well up from all previous years and probably triple the yearly average. Moreover, 58 percent of students were found to have participated, and 75 percent said they agreed with the goals of the protest—a similarly huge increase, if true, from previous years. A similar 75 percent favored "basic changes in the system," 11 percent described themselves as "radical" or "far Left," and 44 per-

Nixon Addresses Antiwar Protestors

Nixon responds to student antiwar demonstrators in a May 8, 1970 press conference.

Question: Mr. President, what do you think the students are trying to say in this demonstration?

The President: They are trying to say that they want peace. They are trying to say that they want to stop the killing. They are trying to say that they want to end the draft. They are trying to say that we ought to get out of Vietnam. I agree with everything that they are trying to accomplish.

I believe, however, that the decisions that I have made, and particularly this last terribly difficult decision of going into the Cambodian sanctuaries which were completely occupied by the enemy—I believe that that decision will serve that purpose, because you can be sure that everything that I stand for is what you want.

I would add this: I think I understand what they want. I would hope they would understand somewhat what I want. When I came to the Presidency—I did not send these men to Vietnam—there were 525,000 men there. And since I have been here, I have been working 18 or 20 hours a day, mostly on Vietnam, trying to bring these men home.

We brought home 115,000. Our casualties were the lowest in the first quarter of this year in 5 years. We are going to bring home another 150,000. And, as a result of the greater accomplishments than we expected in even the first week of the Cambodian campaign, I believe that we will have accomplished our goal of reducing American casualties and, also, of hastening the day that we can have a just peace. But above everything else, to continue the withdrawal program that they are for and that I am for.

Richard Nixon, press conference, May 8, 1970.

cent agreed that social progress was most likely to come from pressures "outside the system."

Public opinion generally also turned sharply against the Nixon administration in the second half of 1970. After the rhetoric of withdrawal, people felt as if they had been duped, more or less the way liberals felt about Lyndon Johnson after the 1964 election. Nixon's approval rating fell below 50 percent for the first time according to Gallup polls; only 38 percent thought he was doing a good job in Vietnam compared to 46 percent who now favored immediate withdrawal. But the Cambodia-related protests occurred, as noted earlier, precisely at a moment when neither radicals nor liberals were organized to take advantage of the welling up of emotion and activism to mold it into something that would endure beyond the passions of the moment. Thus, as it turned out, the 1970 demonstrations were the denouement of the-masses-in-the-streets phase of the antiwar movement. They were a sort of spontaneous conditioned reflex to an extraordinarily crisp and clear escalation of the war in Southeast Asia and on campus. With a single exception, there was not much in the way of large, nationally organized public protest thereafter, and it was not because of students' fear of getting shot.

Nixon Withdraws Troops and Ends the Draft

Rather, the Nixon administration was winding down the ground war, the main killing machine—of Americans at least—in Vietnam; "only" 4,200 U.S. soldiers were killed in Vietnam in 1970, fewer than half the number killed in the previous year, and troop levels were headed down, resting at 334,600 by the end of the year. By the end of 1971, troop strength was down to 156,800—back to 1965 levels—and only about 1,200 were killed during that year. The sensitivity of public opinion to casualties seems to be logarithmic in nature, so that even steady increases in casualties lose their ability to turn people against a war or increase their level of mobilization against it, other factors being equal. How much more unlikely is effective antiwar activism, then, when the casualty rate is decreasing absolutely?

Moreover, the administration's rhetoric was calming. Specifically, on November 12 President Nixon stated publicly that U.S. troops were now limited to a defensive role. More important by far, the pot (bad) luck draft was replaced by a lottery system in early 1970, which eased the psychological strain for many, and in December 1972 President Nixon ended the draft altogether.

As a result of first changing and then ending the draft, Nixon was able to manipulate public opinion about the increased bombing of North Vietnam, which the administration was employing as pressure against Hanoi to negotiate an end to U.S. participation in the war. An April 25, 1972, Gallup poll showed that respondents favored stepped-up bombing by 47 percent against 41 percent, this majority support coming in response partly to a recent North Vietnamese offensive. Clearly, most people did not care as much about how many Asians died in Southeast Asia as they did about the level of U.S. ground combat participation and how many Americans died.

Ending the draft and punching the wind out of the antiwar movement on the one hand, and escalating the air war on the other, was a clever and effective White House tactic. Mike Royko, at the time a pro-war columnist, put it baldly years later:

> . . . in an instant it was over. It was as if someone had flicked a lightswitch. Presto, the throbbing social conscience that had spread across America went limp. The anti-war, pro-peace signs went into the trash bins. Even if you offered free beer and marijuana, you couldn't get enough students together to hold a sit-in. That amazing transformation happened on the day the President

signed into law the end of the draft. At that moment, about 99.9% of those who had sobbed over napalm, Christmas bombings and man's inhumanity to man suddenly began looking for jobs on Wall Street.

Sam Brown put it with more modest candor: "Unfortunately, the end of the draft probably had a substantial impact on the anti-war movement. . . . A lot of high-minded idealists turned out, at least in part, to be interested in self-protection."

Nixon's Tragic Insistence on Peace with Honor

Michael A. Genovese

Nixon's predecessor, Lyndon B. Johnson, had chosen not to run for President in 1968 because he had failed to end American involvement in Vietnam. Nixon did not want to suffer a similar failure. At the same time, however, Nixon believed that America had to act strongly—and achieve a "peace with honor"—in order to discourage aggression in other parts of the world.

In this selection from his book *The Nixon Presidency: Power and Politics in Turbulent Times*, Michael A. Genovese describes Nixon's initial strategy of bombing North Vietnam and mining the important harbor at Haiphong. But in order to bring a close to American involvement in Vietnam, writes Genovese, Nixon and his foreign policy adviser, Henry Kissinger, negotiated a settlement that left South Vietnam at the mercy of the North. Instead of a peace with honor, what resulted was a quick American withdrawal and, ultimately, the invasion and conquest of South Vietnam. Genovese is a professor of political science at Loyola Marymount University.

NIXON'S EFFORTS TO END THE WAR IN VIETNAM MET ONLY with frustration. Hanoi wasn't seriously negotiating, the bombing of the North seemed only to strengthen their resolve, extending the war into Cambodia and Laos had only a limited impact, the antiwar movement seemed to grow

Excerpted from *The Nixon Presidency: Power and Politics in Turbulent Times*, by Michael A. Genovese. Copyright ©1990 by Michael A. Genovese. Reproduced by permission of Greenwood Publishing Group, Inc., Westport, Conn.

larger and angrier with each passing day, and congressional doves seemed always to be undermining the president's position. Would Nixon, like his predecessor, be dragged down and defeated by the Vietnam War? Abroad, Nixon hoped to force the North to negotiate by bombing North Vietnam and Cambodia. At home, Nixon hoped to quell domestic protest by ending the draft, bringing the troops home, and suppressing dissent. Nothing worked as planned.

By 1970, Nixon's initial hope for an early end to the war had vanished. The negotiations between the missions in Paris and between Kissinger and [North Vietnamese negotiator] Le Duc Tho were failing because each side insisted on peace conditions unacceptable to the other. Nixon's alternatives seemed to be either bomb the North to a degree unacceptable by civilized standards, or back away from some of his negotiating demands and hope that Vietnamization would work. But could the president get his much valued "peace with honor" in Vietnam?

In February of 1971, the war expanded further, as South Vietnamese troops, with American air and artillery support, invaded Laos. The goal of the invasion was to invade the Laotian panhandle and defeat the North Vietnamese army at the Ho Chi Minh Trail. But the U.S.-backed forces were trapped inside the Laotian jungle and suffered enormous casualties. It was a military failure in every sense of the word.

As the war dragged on with no honorable end in sight, Nixon began to see Vietnam as a test of his and America's prestige. America would not be "a pitiful, helpless giant," Nixon said; and [Chief of Staff] H.R. Haldeman's notes of meetings with the president reflect a repeated concern for not appearing weak. For example, on June 2, 1971, Haldeman writes:

P. will not go out of VN whimpering
play hole card in Nov - bomb NV totally

unless we get our breakthru
(underlined in original)*

Earlier notes by Haldeman have the president saying, "our purpose is not to defeat <u>NVN—it is to avoid defeat of America</u>" (underlined in original). But "peace with honor" proved no easy goal.

Vietnamization was not working. Nixon could accept defeat or escalate. A summit conference with the Soviet Union was scheduled for May of 1972, and the president was determined to get the Soviets to force North Vietnam to stop the war. Linkage, however, did not work, as the Soviets did not have as much influence over the North Vietnamese as Nixon and Kissinger had, for four years, assumed.

Nixon Says That America Must Be Strong

Le Duc Tho and Henry Kissinger met in Paris. The North was negotiating from a position of strength. Le Duc Tho told Kissinger that he would not compromise. Kissinger returned to the United States with the bad news. In a weekend meeting at Camp David, Nixon decided to escalate. On Monday, May 8, after a lengthy National Security Council meeting at the White House, Nixon handed his own draft of a speech written at Camp David to speechwriter Ray Price. Nixon would go on national television at nine that evening to announce his plans.

"An American defeat in Vietnam," Nixon said, "would encourage . . . aggression all over the world. . . . I have . . . concluded that Hanoi must be denied the weapons and supplies it needs to continue the aggression." He continued, "All entrances to North Vietnamese ports will be mined to prevent access to these ports and North Vietnamese naval operations from these ports."

----

*Editor's Note: This should be read: President will not go out of Vietnam whimpering. Play ace in the hole card in November—bomb North Vietnam totally.

The North was to be blockaded. The air force would bomb rail and roadways, along with military targets in the North. The bombing of Hanoi and Haiphong began immediately. In an effort to create the appearance of public support for these actions, the Committee to Re-elect the President spent eight thousand dollars to have false letters and telegrams of support sent to the White House.

Under the grueling pressure of round-the-clock bombing (Nixon said to his associates, "The bastards have never been bombed like they're going to be bombed this time"), the North finally agreed to return to the negotiating table. In the summer of 1972, as a presidential election was approaching, the two sides met in Paris.

Attention turned to Paris and the negotiations to end the war. As the negotiations progressed, the bombings decreased. In a frantic, often confusing and contradictory process of proposal and counterproposal, Henry Kissinger kept working for an honorable way out of the war. But the North Vietnamese wanted a negotiated victory. A two-track American process of negotiation and bombing continued in the hope of driving the North to an agreement more amenable to American interests.

Negotiating Away South Vietnam

By the early summer of 1972, North Vietnam's politburo made a breakthrough concession. They would drop their demand for a coalition government in the South. Thieu would be permitted to remain in office. In effect, the North was agreeing to let the United States leave Vietnam and to wait for either the government of the South to collapse or an opportunity to overthrow a shaky government with a questionable military capacity. From that point on, the negotiations moved ahead. By the fall of 1972, an agreement was in sight. A cease-fire was agreed to, the North was allowed to keep its troops in the South (a major concession by Nixon), all U.S. troops were to withdraw, a government

Nixon Claims to Have
Achieved Peace with Honor

After the withdrawal from Vietnam, Nixon's advisers tried to depict the president as a successful peacemaker.

Realizing as early as January 9, 1973, that they had failed to create a "just and lasting peace," Nixon and his aides discussed the problem of countering skeptics and influencing the verdict of history. Drafted by speech writer Patrick J. Buchanan, the White House plan aimed at portraying Nixon as the leading "peacemaker" in a long war. It would obfuscate details, build on the emerging body of "revisionist" writing that was defending the war, and target the press, scholars, and the public. The plan had four multipart messages. First, with the support of the silent majority and his friends in Congress, the president had had the courage, toughness, and wisdom to make the hard decisions and see them through—despite unprecedented attacks from critics in Congress and the media. Second, no quarter was to be given to opponents, especially those on Capitol Hill, whose criticisms and resolutions against the war had prolonged the conflict. Many in Congress would have simply withdrawn U.S. troops from Vietnam in exchange for POWs (prisoners of war), which was nothing more than a plan for cutting and running, the equivalent of abject, dishonorable defeat and surrender. It would also have led to a bloodbath of continued war, in which the 50 million long-suffering people of Indochina would have had to fight on without the United States. The critics were wrong, therefore, and Nixon was right.

Third, "our" peace with a cease-fire was not a "bug out" but one that achieved the major goals of the war: It got our POWs back, won "peace with independence for South Vietnam and peace for the people of Southeast Asia," and assured the right of the South Vietnamese to determine their own future without the communists imposing a government on them. Furthermore, despite the unpopularity of the war and the mistakes made by previous administrations in fighting it, the president's handling of it preserved the credibility of the U.S. commitment, "which is essential not only to our national self-respect but to our continuing role as a force for peace in the world." Fourth, certain misconceptions had to be shot down: It was not possible to settle on a peace in December; the peace agreement signed in January could not have been had earlier; the January agreement was an improvement over the October peace agreement; the Vietnamese [National Council of Reconciliation and Concord] (NCRC) was not a "coalition" government; the Thieu government had not been abandoned; there was never any division between the president and Kissinger. As for the December blitz over Hanoi, Buchanan's document elaborated, it was not "terror bombing" but struck only military targets; it broke the deadlock in negotiations, forced the other side back to the table, and won concessions from them while protecting the sovereignty of South Vietnam and winning the release of U.S. POWs. It had, in other words, won a peace with honor. His diplomacy of threats having failed to achieve a real victory as he had originally defined it, Richard Nixon's Vietnam diplomacy was now aimed primarily at public, scholarly, and international opinion in a battle of symbolism, rhetoric, and interpretation.

Jeffrey P. Kimball, "Peace with Honor: Richard Nixon and the Diplomacy of Threat and Symbolism," in David L. Anderson, ed., *Shadow on the White House*, Kansas City: University Press of Kansas, 1993.

that included communists was established, and an election commission was set up to decide the fate of Vietnam.

South Vietnam was not a party to this agreement, and when Henry Kissinger took the tentative agreement to South Vietnam's president Thieu in October, things began to fall apart. Thieu correctly recognized that the agreement was South Vietnam's death warrant. He refused to allow the North's troops, numbering around 145,000 to remain in the South and refused to recognize the legitimacy of the Vietcong.

Nixon and Kissinger pressed Thieu, telling him that this was the best they could do and promising continued support to Thieu. On October 26, 1972, Radio Hanoi disclosed the terms of the agreement in hopes of forcing the United States to sign the agreement. Also on October 26, Henry Kissinger announced at a press conference that "peace is at hand." This premature announcement, less than two weeks before the 1972 presidential election, blew up in Kissinger's face. Thieu refused to accept the deal struck by Kissinger and Le Duc Tho. Kissinger urged Nixon to make a separate peace agreement with Hanoi, but Nixon refused.

Kissinger and Le Duc Tho met in mid-November of 1972 to try once again to iron out an agreement, but the introduction of President Thieu's demands led to North Vietnamese objections. Things seemed to be going in reverse. In an effort to get an agreement, Nixon informed the North that if Thieu remained intransigent, he would make a separate deal with Hanoi; further he threatened Thieu with a cutoff of U.S. support if Thieu refused to go along with the agreement. Nixon also promised Thieu that if the North violated the agreement, the United States would "save" South Vietnam from a communist takeover. Finally, Nixon gave Hanoi seventy-two hours to seriously resume negotiations or face renewed, and more-massive, B-52 bombing of the North.

The Christmas Bombing and Nixon's Ungraceful Peace

Nixon decided to step up the pressure. On December 18, 1972, U.S. B-52s began a twelve-day, round-the-clock bombing of North Vietnam in which the United States dropped more tons of bombs than had been dropped in the entire 1969–71 period. The "Christmas Bombing" shocked the nation and the world. It was one of the most brutal examples of force in history. It was an effort to bomb the North into submission. As the bombs showered the North, Nixon sweetened the pot for Thieu and the South, giving them an additional billion dollars in military aid while warning Thieu that if he didn't accept the American "peace" terms, Nixon would make his own peace with North Vietnam. In the end, neither side could resist Nixon's ultimatum.

The North returned to the bargaining table, Nixon ordered a halt to the bombing, Thieu acquiesced to American pressures and promises, and in Paris on January 23, 1973, the Agreement on Ending the War and Restoring Peace in Vietnam was initialed by Henry Kissinger and Le Duc Tho. Nixon claimed his "peace with honor."

Twenty-seven months after the signing of the Paris accords, the Saigon government fell to the communists, in spite of Nixon's promise to President Thieu to "respond with full force" if the North violated the agreements (Nixon told Thieu in March of 1973, "You can count on us"). Nixon had been forced from office, and America had no stomach for a return to Vietnam. The North had conquered the South by force. The Khmer Rouge controlled Cambodia.

At a January 31, 1973, press conference announcing the peace agreement, Nixon took a swipe at the press. Against great odds, we had, Nixon said, achieved "peace with honor"; "I know it gags some of you to write that phrase, but it is true, and most Americans realize it is true."

In their memoirs, Nixon and Kissinger defended their conduct during the Vietnam War and blamed Congress and the media for the 1975 fall of Saigon. While the Congress, much of the press, and a majority of the public *did* oppose the war, shifting blame to others for a failed policy in Vietnam only obscures the issue. For nearly twenty years the United States acted in Vietnam on false assumptions and incomplete information. There is enough blame to spread around. American policy in Vietnam was doomed because our operating assumptions were almost always wrong. Richard Nixon inherited a war that he expanded, then ended on terms that were bound to collapse. For America, and for Southeast Asia, the Vietnam War was a tragic mistake and a tragic failure. And for Nixon, actions stemming from that war led to his own downfall. In the end, Nixon's goal of military victory in Vietnam gave way to hopes for a negotiated settlement, which gave way to a turning of the war over to South Vietnam, which gave way to hopes of peace with honor, which finally gave way to U.S. withdrawal without humiliation. But in the end, not only did South Vietnam and Cambodia fall, but Nixon also fell victim to the war. As a direct result of actions taken stemming from the war, the seeds of Watergate were planted. Nixon thus became yet another victim of the tragedy of Vietnam.

PRESIDENTS
and their
DECISIONS

NIXON'S VISIT
TO CHINA

Nixon's Opening of China Was a Major Accomplishment

Cecil V. Crabb Jr.

Richard Nixon was president during the Cold War, when the United States claimed responsibility for preventing the spread of communism in the world. Since 1949, when Communists had gained control of China, U.S.–Chinese relations had been very tense. For example, China had supported American enemies in both Korea and Vietnam. In a policy known as containment, the United States worked to prevent the spread of communism from China to other East Asian nations. In addition, the United States refused to recognize the Communist regime in China and, instead supporting the Nationalist Chinese regime, which had been defeated by the Communists in 1949 and forced into exile on the island Taiwan.

However, as Cecil V. Crabb Jr. points out in his book *American Foreign Policy in the Nuclear Age*, by the early 1970s enough time had passed that the countries could once again understand each other in terms of interests rather than ideologies. Such interests, Crabb notes, included the power of the Soviet Union, America's role in East Asia, Japan, and Taiwan. When Nixon became president, he visited China and, in communicating about their shared interests, was able to help "normalize" relations between the two nations. Crabb is a professor of political science at Louisiana State University and the author of many books on American foreign policy.

Excerpted from *American Foreign Policy in the Nuclear Age*, 5th ed., by Cecil V. Crabb Jr. Copyright ©1988 by Harper & Row, Publishers, Inc. Reprinted by permission of Addison Wesley Educational Publishers Inc.

BEFORE ANY FUNDAMENTAL CHANGE IN THE COURSE OF Sino-American relations was possible, three preconditions had to be met. One was that a prolonged period of time had to elapse, enabling both countries to outgrow the attitudes of mutual suspicion and antagonism that accompanied the Communist victory in China. Another prerequisite was that China had to break out of the Soviet orbit and pursue its own independent foreign policy goals. Finally, the prolonged and costly war in Vietnam had to be brought to an end. By the early 1970s, all of these requirements had substantially been fulfilled. (If the Vietnam conflict had not officially ended, its outcome was evident, and initial steps had been taken in arriving at a cease-fire agreement.)

Ironically, it was the Republican Administration of President Richard M. Nixon—whose supporters had long condemned earlier Democratic administrations for having "lost China" to communism—that began the process of normalizing relations between the United States and the People's Republic of China. Early in 1970, Nixon's national security adviser, Henry Kissinger, responded to an overture from Chinese officials in Warsaw presaging a new era in Sino-American relations. As Kissinger later assessed the matter, "For twenty years, US policymakers considered China as a brooding, chaotic, fanatical, and alien realm difficult to comprehend and impossible to sway." Long-standing mutual suspicions between the two countries had made their relations sterile and unproductive. But by the early 1970s, officials in both countries "dimly perceived [the emergence of a] community of interest between the United States and China." For the first time since 1949, Kissinger believed, the leaders of both countries had begun "to regard each other in geopolitical rather than ideological terms."

After a complex series of preliminary meetings and negotiations—including a secret visit to Peking by Kissinger early in July 1971—President Nixon electrified the world by announcing that he intended to visit the People's Republic of China. On February 17, 1972, Nixon left Washington for a state visit to mainland China. During this historic visit (the first by an American president to China), discussions between officials of the two countries ranged over a wide variety of major and minor issues—from American and Chinese assessments of Soviet intentions to "ping-pong diplomacy" and other forms of cultural contact between the two countries, to expanded Sino-American economic and commercial relations.

Important Issues in Chinese-American Relations

Several fundamental questions of mutual interest were at the forefront of Sino-American concern. A dominant one was Chinese and American assessments of Soviet diplomatic behavior and the proper response to it. Confronted with ongoing hostility from Moscow, and with a formidable Soviet military machine along its more than 4,500-mile border, China looked to American power to counterbalance the superior might of its principal adversary. If Peking did not propose, or even realistically expect, that the United States was prepared to become a formal military ally of China against the Soviet Union, it was nevertheless hoped that a normalization of Sino-American relations would serve as a deterrent to Soviet expansionist tendencies in Asia.

A related issue was the role of the United States in Asia after the Vietnam War. Despite their earlier opposition to American intervention in Southeast Asia, Chinese officials left little doubt that they counted upon an active and influential role by the United States within Asia after the Vietnam conflict. In opposition to some critics of American involvement in the war, Peking did *not* call for or seek an American withdrawal from the region. To the contrary, in Chinese eyes, the power of the United States served as a necessary counterweight to two actual or potential tendencies inimical to the security and diplomatic interests of China. One was the ongoing buildup of *Soviet military power* in Asia in the post–Vietnam War era. The other was *the resurgence of Japanese power and influence* within the region. While the PRC did not necessarily oppose the latter development—and the Chinese government in fact looked to Japan for economic assistance and investment—it did rely upon the United States to curb any new Japanese imperial impulse.

Nixon Changes the World

In his memoirs, Nixon recalled the significance of his joint communiqué with Chinese leaders. The message to the world was that these two superpowers would now get along openly.

In my toast at the banquet on our last night in China I said, "The joint communiqué which we have issued today summarizes the results of our talks. That communiqué will make headlines around the world tomorrow. But what we have said in that communiqué is not nearly as important as what we will do in the years ahead to build a bridge across 16,000 miles and twenty-two years of hostility which have divided us in the past."

I raised my glass and said, "We have been here a week. This was the week that changed the world."

Richard Nixon, *The Memoirs of Richard Nixon.* New York: Grossett and Dunlap, 1978.

For over two decades, the most difficult and controversial issue confronting the United States and Communist China was the future of Taiwan and America's close military and diplomatic ties with it; that question had lost none of its complexity with the passage of time. The Chinese view—and a position held among the Chinese on Taiwan and on the mainland alike—was that Taiwan was *an integral part of China.* Washington viewed the Republic of China on Formosa as an independent, non-Communist government, with which it maintained cordial ties, formal diplomatic relations, and firm military links (expressed in the American-Taiwan defense treaty of 1955). American officials opposed any attempt by Communist China to liberate Taiwan by force. During President Nixon's visit, officials of the two countries thoroughly reviewed the Taiwan question, reiterated their respective positions, and in effect "agreed to disagree" about their viewpoints toward it. In brief, the troublesome Taiwan issue was left officially unresolved.

Both China and America Gained by Nixon's Attempt to Establish Normal Relations

Robert G. Sutter

When Nixon took office, the United States and China did not share normal diplomatic relations, and had not since 1949, the year that China became a Communist state known as the People's Republic of China under Chairman Mao Zedong. China had also been prevented from joining the United Nations, and as a result had spent many years in diplomatic isolation. U.S.–Chinese relations were especially bad because of Chinese support for Communist regimes in the Soviet Union, North Korea, and North Vietnam.

In this selection, Robert G. Sutter points out that leaders in both countries were extremely bold, since they had much to lose. The status of Taiwan—where Mao's enemies, supported by the United States, had settled—was especially problematic. Nonetheless, the two nations chose to move forward because of the many potential benefits of normal diplomatic relations. China stood to gain a more comfortable role in East Asia as well as a balance against the Soviet Union. The United States also sought strategic advantages. According to Sutter, the ability of leaders in both countries to get past their disagreements was a positive step forward for the global balance of power. Robert G. Sutter is chief of the Foreign Affairs and National Defense Division and a senior specialist in international policy with the Congressional Research Service.

Excerpted from *Cold War Patriot and Statesman: Richard M. Nixon*, edited by Leon Friedman and William F. Levantrosser. Copyright ©1993 by Hofstra University. Reproduced by permission of Greenwood Publishing Group, Inc., Westport, Conn.

T HE SECRET DIPLOMATIC OPENING TO CHINA CONDUCTED by President Richard Nixon and his national security adviser Henry Kissinger was a bold and successful stroke that transformed, to American advantage, the Asian balance. In retrospect, it seems to have been a natural step. But this view ignores the three less recognized perspectives that emphasize the risks, the gambles, and the vision of the administration's action:

- First, the tenuous position of those in China with whom President Nixon and Henry Kissinger were negotiating;
- second, the long history of American unwillingness to recognize and take advantage of the potential for an important convergence of interests of the Chinese Communist movement and the United States in the Asian balance of power; and
- third, the dangers and pitfalls of using secret diplomacy to transform key features of American foreign policy. . . .

One of the marks of great statesmen is the capacity to seize opportunities created by changing and seemingly adverse circumstances. Such boldness characterized President Richard Nixon, Henry Kissinger, and Chinese leaders Mao Zedong and Zhou Enlai, when they broke through decades of hostility and distrust to establish a Sino-American understanding in the mutual interests of their countries. The historical record shows that the leaders were not motivated in this endeavor by romantic fascination, ideology, or perceived commercial advantage. Rather, it was their clear view of changing international circumstances, relating particularly to the balance of power in Asia, that persuaded Chinese and U.S. leaders that their nations' well-being and their own political standing would be best served by improved Sino-American understanding.

The rapprochement with the United States achieved during President Richard M. Nixon's February 1972 visit marks China's most important success in realigning the Asian balance of power in modem times. In the late 1960s, Chinese leaders became increasingly aware of China's vulnerable strategic position. That vulnerability stemmed in part from disruptions of China's military preparedness during the Cultural Revolution, and it was enhanced by significantly greater Soviet military power deployed along the Chinese frontier. But at its heart lay Beijing's strident opposition to both superpowers.

The August 1968 Soviet incursion into Czechoslovakia and Moscow's concurrent formulation of the so-called Brezhnev Doctrine of limited sovereignty demonstrated to the Chinese that Moscow might be prepared to use overwhelming military superiority in order to pressure, and even to invade, the People's Republic of China (PRC). The Sino-Soviet border clashes of 1969 increased Beijing's concern over the Soviet threat. In response, Chinese officials—under the leadership of Mao Zedong and Zhou Enlai—began a major effort in 1969 to broaden Beijing's leverage against the Soviet Union by ending China's international isolation. In this pursuit, they utilized conventional diplomacy and played down the ideological shrillness characteristic of Chinese foreign policy during the earlier stages of the Cultural Revolution.

Because of Moscow's massive power, Beijing realized that improving diplomatic and other relations with most foreign nations would be of relatively minor significance in helping China with its pressing need to offset the USSR. In East Asia, only the other superpower, the United States, seemed to have sufficient strength to serve as an effective deterrent to Soviet pressure. In the past Moscow had shown uneasiness over signs of possible reconciliation between China and the United States. Thus, the Chinese leaders were aware that they held an important option: they could move closer to the United States in order to readjust Sino-Soviet relations and form a new balance of power in East Asia more favorable to Chinese interests.

Although the Chinese faced increasingly heavy Soviet pressure in 1969, the newly installed Nixon Administration was beginning policy initiatives designed to pull back American military forces from Asia and to reduce U.S. commitments along the periphery of China. It was soon apparent that the policy of gradual troop withdrawal, part of the later-named Nixon Doctrine, was perceived favorably by Beijing. The Chinese leaders saw the American pullback as solid evidence of the Nixon Administration's avowed interest in improved relations with China. They also viewed it as a major opportunity for China to free itself from the burdensome task of maintaining an extensive defense network along China's southern and eastern borders against possible U.S.–backed armed incursions. Beijing now saw greater opportunity for China to spread its own influence in neighboring East Asian areas as the United States gradually retreated.

Primarily on the basis of these two factors—a need to use Sino-American rapprochement to offset Soviet pressure on China and a desire to take advantage of prospects opening for the PRC under terms of the Nixon Doctrine in Asia—Beijing agreed to receive President Nixon and to begin the process of normalizing Sino-American relations. Although the joint communiqué signed by Nixon and Zhou Enlai in Shanghai in February 1972 acknowledged major differences between the two sides over ideology, Taiwan, and several foreign policy issues, it showed that they had reached an important agreement on what principles should govern the future international order in East Asia. In particular, both sides agreed that they would not seek hegemony in the Asia-Pacific region and would oppose efforts by any other country to establish hegemony there.

This accord served China's interests well. For the previous two decades, Beijing had existed within a generally hostile East Asia environment and had periodically faced threats to its national security. The Sino-American rapprochement presented Beijing with an opportunity for a more relaxed stance on its eastern and southern flanks. It also provided major support for China against Soviet pressure. Support from the United States for the so-called antihegemony clause in the Shanghai Communiqué represented for China an important strategic statement. It put Washington on record as opposing any effort by Moscow to dominate China, and it made it possible for Beijing to relax its vigilance on the eastern and southern flanks and concentrate on the north.

Good Chinese-American Relations Were More Important than Anti-Communism

The Chinese-American agreement also conformed with U.S. strategic interests. By the late 1960s, the cost and futility of massive U.S. military involvement in Vietnam had vividly demonstrated the limitations of the American use of force to counter what Washington had previously viewed as the strategic threat of international communism. The experience forced Washington to reassess the prevailing international order in light of its newly perceived weakness. Over the previous decade, while the United States had become increasingly involved in Vietnam, the Soviet Union had drawn abreast of the United States in strategic weapons. During the previous twenty years, the United States had enjoyed strategic superiority and commensurate international influence, allowing it to pursue an ideological campaign against international communism and to support the free world. Washington now realized that it could no longer afford such a policy. In particular, it saw that the United States could no longer, on its own, sustain the balance of forces on continental Asia.

Thus, the United States, under the Nixon Administration, began to put aside past, undifferentiated prejudice against Communist regimes in general and to actively capitalize on nationalist divergencies in Asia, hoping thereby to achieve a more favorable strategic balance. The major divergence Washington chose to exploit was that between Moscow and Beijing. The United States realized that, by withdrawing from forward military positions along China's periphery—a move that would conserve American resources for use in support of more important interests against Moscow—it could reach agreement with Beijing and possibly establish a more favorable equilibrium in the area.

At the same time, the president and his advisers were anxious to use perceived international leverage derived from the opening of China in order to elicit greater accommodations from the Soviet Union over pressing international and arms control issues; and from Communist Vietnam over conditions for a peace settlement. The president was also motivated by the prospect of personal political benefits from success in improving U.S. relations, on generally favorable terms, with a heretofore hostile China.

Brave Leadership in Both China and the United States

Since the benefits of Sino–U.S. rapprochement now seem so clear, it is reasonable to ask why U.S. and Chinese leaders did not act earlier. This clarity of hindsight, however, greatly underplays the bold accomplishments of U.S. and Chinese leaders.

Such an assessment ignores the substantial risk of failure the leaders on both sides took in their efforts to improve relations. Ideological and systematic differences, domestic politics, and differences in international strategy made the Sino-American policy an extremely sensitive topic in both capitals. Thus, President Nixon had to take careful account of the legacy of past emotional and partisan debates on U.S.–China policy; the need to preserve unity within his own conservative political constituency; and the imperatives of confidentiality in delicate interaction with a heretofore hostile adversary. Although the president made clear his desire for better relations with China and took some public steps designed to ease tensions and improve ties, he felt compelled to keep secret his efforts aimed at a breakthrough until Henry Kissinger completed his secret trip to Beijing in July 1971.

Analysts of Chinese affairs point out that the stakes in the policy debate in China at this time were even higher. Moves by Zhou Enlai and his associates to improve relations with the United States during 1968–71 had produced vigorous criticism from Zhou's rivals. Such internal opposition, for example, had forced Zhou and his associates to drop, just before a scheduled Warsaw meeting, an initiative to explore the new Nixon Administration's intentions in February 1969.

This was a period of intense leadership conflict in the PRC. It subsided only with the death of Defense Minister Lin Piao and his family in September 1971 and the arrest and detention of the main leaders of the Chinese Military High Command. These events came just two months after Kissinger's secret visit to Beijing.

Officials associated with Lin, through speeches and commentary in the Chinese media, had made known their opposition to the opening to the United States. The success of Zhou's opening to the United States presumably was an important factor in his ability and that of his followers to win the life and death struggle for power with Lin Piao and his associates then underway in Beijing. Had the opening to the United States failed, it is safe to conclude, Zhou's fate and that of his followers might have been quite different.

Nixon's Withdrawal from Vietnam Made His Opening of China Possible

Joseph Camilleri

From the late 1940s until Nixon's presidency, American foreign policy was built around an idea known as containment. Americans believed that they needed to contain communism to the countries which already practiced it, and prevent its spread to new countries. A nation that had to be isolated, according to this policy, was the People's Republic of China, Communist since 1949. In addition, containment required that South Vietnam be protected from a Communist takeover.

In his book *Chinese Foreign Policy: The Maoist Era and Its Aftermath*, from which the following selection is excerpted, Joseph Camilleri suggests that China was only willing to open its relations with the United States when Nixon abandoned the policy of containment with regard to both China and Vietnam. The Chinese, he asserts, would not speak to Nixon or to his national security adviser Henry Kissinger until they began to withdraw troops from Vietnam. Camilleri points out also that it was the Chinese who gained most from the normalization of relations, since with his visit Nixon acknowledged that China was a major power in East Asia and a leader of the Third World. Joseph Camilleri is a professor of politics at Latrobe University.

Excerpted from *Chinese Foreign Policy: The Maoist Era and Its Aftermath*, by Joseph Camilleri (Seattle: University of Washington Press, 1990). Copyright ©1990 by Joseph Camilleri. Reprinted by permission of the author.

U NDOUBTEDLY THE SINGLE MOST IMPORTANT FACTOR contributing to the Nixon changes in American policy towards China was the profound disenchantment with the Vietnam War. In its initial stages, United States military intervention in Vietnam was conceived as an integral part of the policy of containment and had the support of the majority of the American public. Yet within a few years it became evident that this military adventure would exact a heavy toll in men, money and prestige. Apart from causing widespread anxiety and frustration within the American body politic, the costly and ever-expanding conflict inevitably produced despondency, dissent and mass desertions in the American armed forces. Calls for an end to the bombing and the withdrawal of American troops from Vietnam eventually resulted in a series of congressional initiatives to end the fighting and restrict the powers of the President.

As a consequence of the Vietnam experience, the United States was now much more inclined to reduce its military presence in Asia and to move towards a policy that accepted, however grudgingly, the end of the post-war era of exclusive American hegemony over the non-Communist world. By the late 1960s, the intellectual elite and the public at large, as well as a large cross-section of congressional opinion, were ready to replace the bipolar conception of international relations with a more flexible notion of multipolar relationships. By accepting the emergence of China as a great power, whose interests had to be given due consideration, American diplomacy was perhaps hoping that a tacit agreement might be reached between the two countries about their respective spheres of influence. Such an understanding might permit the United States to pursue its policy of military disengagement in Indochina in the knowledge that its political and economic dominance in other parts of Asia would not, as a consequence, be subjected to serious challenge.

Indeed, some observers have argued that President Nixon's underlying objective in fostering the Sino-American rapprochement was to persuade Peking to use all its influence on Hanoi so that American troops might be withdrawn from Vietnam with minimum humiliation to the United States and with sufficient concessions from Communist forces in Indochina to allow a political solution to the war compatible with American interests. The Nixon administration may also have entertained the hope that, in return for closer relations with the United States, China would terminate, or at least significantly reduce, her support for insurgency operations and liberation movements in Southeast Asia. There is, however, no evidence to suggest that such an understanding was ever reached, explicitly or even tacitly, between the two countries. China, for her part, consistently maintained that the withdrawal of American forces from the whole of Indochina would, at least in principle, have to precede normalization of Sino-American relations.

Even if one were to overlook China's ideological commitment to the revolutionary struggle in Indochina, Nixon's meandering Vietnam policy would still have remained unacceptable to Peking for security reasons, at least so long as the United States retained in the area the kind of military presence that threatened to unleash a larger confrontation and precipitate China's more direct involvement. Throughout 1970 and the early months of 1971, official Chinese statements continued to describe the American escalation of the war as a threat to the security of the People's Republic and to the peace of Asia and the world. A Sino-Vietnamese communiqué issued in March 1971 reaffirmed in the strongest possible terms China's opposition to American actions in Indochina. As already indicated, such statements were intended primarily to deter the United States from expanding the ground war rather than to set the stage for China's direct military intervention. In other words, the warnings issued by Peking during this period were concerned much more with a potential rather than an actual threat.

The Chinese Were Reassured by Nixon's Withdrawal of Troops from Vietnam

In any case, the anxieties experienced by the Maoist leadership with regard to Chinese security were to some extent allayed by the series of messages delivered from Washington to the Chinese government through various diplomatic intermediaries. According to one well-informed observer, the purport of these communications was to assure China of President Nixon's "new outlook" on Asia and of his determination to withdraw from Vietnam as quickly as possible, while seeking a negotiated settlement of the conflict. An even more important factor in dissipating Chinese fears was the actual process of withdrawal. By August 1969 the departure of the first 25,000 troops from South Vietnam had been completed, and by November 1971 only 196,000 troops remained compared with a peak of 543,000 in February 1969. If the United States had not succeeded in winning the war when its armed strength was at its height, it could scarcely hope to do so with a much reduced military capability. In this sense, the Vietnamization policy was a poorly executed attempt to disguise the inevitable defeat and translate the belated realization that no Saigon army, however well equipped, could withstand for long the tide of popular opposition or the advancing Communist forces. Having sought an illusory military victory for nearly a decade, American strategy now had to concede that the Communists had won the decisive political battle in the struggle for the liberation and reunification of Vietnam.

By the middle of 1971, if not earlier, Peking was probably convinced that the United States was finally getting out of Vietnam, although Washington's last minute attempts to find a face-saving formula for a while prolonged the fighting and postponed the Communist victory. Once the Chinese leadership made up its mind that American diplomacy was reconciled to its defeat in Indochina, the movement towards a Sino-American détente gathered considerable momentum. Accordingly, on 17 July 1971 came the historic announcement that President Nixon would visit China before May 1972, and that his National Security Adviser, Dr. Kissinger, who had been reported to be indisposed in Pakistan, was actually in Peking conferring with [Chinese Premier] Zhou Enlai. The joint statement announcing the forthcoming visit by the American head of state made it clear that the initiative for the invitation had come from President Nixon himself. There is reason to believe that the White House had made use of the good offices of several well-placed third parties, notably France and Pakistan, to indicate its interest in holding high-level discussions with the Chinese leadership. In the July statement, the two purposes of the Nixon visit were specified as the normalization of relations and an exchange of views on questions of mutual concern. Following a second visit to Peking by Dr. Kissinger in October 1971 and several months of consultations, it was finally agreed on 30 November that President Nixon would set off for his historic journey to China on 21 February 1972.

Nixon in China

While the seven days the American President and his entourage spent in Peking may not have changed the world, they certainly consummated one of the most dramatic shifts in United States foreign policy since World War II. The joint communiqué issued at Shanghai on 27 February revealed little of the "serious and frank exchange of views", which took place behind closed doors and covered the whole range of bilateral and international issues. Nevertheless, enough was disclosed to indicate the radical transformation of the Sino-American relationship. Apart from the specific agreements reached with regard to the further development of contacts and exchanges in science, technology, culture, sports and journalism, and the facilitation of bilateral trade, the two sides agreed to maintain close diplomatic contact through various channels, "including the sending of a senior US representative to Peking from time to time for concrete consultations to further the normalization of relations." Equally significant was the willingness of the United States to identify with China's formulation of the five principles of peaceful coexistence:

> ... countries, regardless of their social systems, should conduct their relations on the principles of respect for the sovereignty and territorial integrity of all states, non-aggression against other states, non-interference in the internal affairs of other states, equality and mutual benefit, and peaceful coexistence. International disputes should be settled on this basis without resorting to the use or threat of force.

Indeed, the statement went a long way towards accepting the need to limit great power interests and spheres of influence:

> • both [China and the United States] wish to reduce the danger of international military conflict;
>
> • neither should seek hegemony in the Asia-Pacific region and each is opposed to efforts by any other country or group of countries to establish such hegemony ...

It is of course more than likely that neither China nor the United States was altogether sincere in renouncing great power ambitions. Regardless of their real intentions, the statement nevertheless constituted an implicit repudiation of American behaviour, which had attempted to construct over a period of two decades an overwhelming military presence stretching in an unbroken semicircle from Japan to Thailand, for the explicit purpose of containing

China and maintaining in power a loose coalition of anti-Communist client states. In China's case, the statement reinforced her claim that she would never be a superpower, that she harboured no great power ambitions, and that she belonged to the Third World through both circumstance and choice. Moreover, this public affirmation of principle underlined China's revolutionary credentials, in particular her recognition of the right of any nation to make its own revolution, and, more importantly, her opposition to the attempts of any great power to frustrate such a revolution.

On the question of Taiwan, the two parties found it necessary to present separate statements of their respective positions. China, for her part, restated her traditional demands:

> The Taiwan question is the crucial question obstructing the normalization of relations between China and the United States; the Government of the People's Republic of China is the sole legal government of China; Taiwan is a province of China . . . the liberation of Taiwan is China's internal affair . . . all U.S. forces and military installations must be withdrawn from Taiwan.

In the case of the United States, there was a clear departure from previously established policy:

> The United States acknowledges that all Chinese on either side of the Taiwan Strait maintain that there is but one China and that Taiwan is part of China. The U.S. government does not challenge that position. It reaffirms its interest in a peaceful settlement of the Taiwan question by the Chinese themselves. With this prospect in mind, it affirms the ultimate objective of the withdrawal of all U.S. forces and military installations from Taiwan. In the meantime, it will progressively reduce its forces and military installations on Taiwan as the tension in the area diminishes.

Implicit in this declaration was the American acceptance of the principle of "one China", although its realization was left to an unspecified future date. It is worth noting, in this respect, that, while China did not denounce the US-Taiwan treaty, the United States did not reaffirm its commitment to it. The unstated assumption of the American position was that the Taiwan problem would gradually fade away to the advantage of Peking as a result of the phased withdrawal of the American military and diplomatic support that the Chiang Kai-shek regime had enjoyed since 1949.

China Was Acknowledged to Be a Dominant Power

The net effect of the American presidential visit and the ensuing diplomatic, scientific, cultural and trade agreements was to enhance China's prestige as a great power and consolidate the diplomatic successes she had achieved since the Cultural Revolution. As for the United States, the new dialogue with China formally spelled the end of the containment policy, at least as it had been applied in Asia since 1950, and a re-evaluation of China's role in the international political system. In the words of Marshall Green, speaking before a congressional sub-committee in May 1972:

> . . . in the coming decade China will play a key role in events in Asia and will have a major part in shaping its future. Indeed, its voice will increasingly be heard also in world councils.

Apart from a few pockets of right-wing dissent, the shift in American diplomacy gained widespread approval within the United States. As one would expect, the reaction of most Third World countries and the whole of Western Europe was also positive. Many of these governments had for a long time been advocating a reassessment of American attitudes towards Maoist China. Nevertheless, the reaction of some Asian governments, especially those that depended for their continued existence on US military support, was one of apprehension and, at least in one instance, of outright opposition. The sharp denunciations emanating from Taibei [Taipei] in the wake of the Nixon visit to Peking left little doubt that the Taiwan government was deeply dismayed by the long-term implications of Washington's new China policy.

In order to dispel some of the concerns and misgivings of these governments, the American President sent Marshall Green and a senior staff member of the National Security Council on a tour of thirteen Asian countries to explain and justify the apparent discontinuity in American foreign policy. But no new assurances, however firm, could easily erase the credibility gap that had arisen in America's relations with client Asian states. It was precisely the Asian appreciation of the gradual decline of the American empire that now predisposed even some of the most fiercely anti-Communist governments to seek an accommodation with the People's Republic and their other Communist neighbours. China had finally won regional acceptance of her dominant role in Asia as well as universal recognition of her vastly enhanced status in the emerging global balance of power.

NIXON'S POLICY TOWARD CHINA WAS SELF-SERVING

GEORGE W. BALL

By the early 1970s, Americans had grown tired of their involvement in Vietnam. On the other side of the Pacific, the Chinese had suffered through a brutal Cultural Revolution and were growing concerned over the Soviet Union, with whom they shared a border. Richard Nixon was able to take advantage of these fortunate historical circumstances to "open" China.

However, in this selection from his book *Diplomacy for a Crowded World*, George W. Ball claims that Nixon should be criticized for conducting his China policy in secret before finally announcing his visit to China in February 1972. Not only was this a betrayal of Japan and other American allies, writes Ball, it also allowed Nixon to turn his visit to China into a public relations ploy.

Ball was undersecretary of state during parts of the Kennedy and Johnson administrations. In 1968 he also served briefly as the U.S. ambassador to the United Nations.

N O EPISODE IN THE NIXON ADMINISTRATION HAS BEEN more praised or misunderstood—or, indeed, misrepresented—than the President's visit to China. Contrary to the manner in which it was presented to the American people, it was by no means an intricate diplomatic maneuver or a triumph of negotiation. The Chinese did not have to be persuaded to open their doors; they had their own

Excerpted from *Diplomacy for a Crowded World*, by George Ball. Copyright ©1976 by George W. Ball. Reprinted by permission of Little, Brown and Company, Inc.

strategic reasons for wishing to resume communications with the United States and they were making that point loudly and clearly. . . .

With China bracketed on the north by an increasingly bellicose Soviet Union and on the south by an India that seemed to be slipping more and more toward Moscow, [Chinese leader] Mao Tse-tung and his colleagues were encouraged to reassess their position toward the United States. Fear of America generated by our march to the Yalu in October 1950, and regenerated by our swelling deployments in Southeast Asia in the 1960s, abated once the United States began the long process of withdrawal from Vietnam. The coincidence of three events—President Johnson's speech in March 1968, halting the further extension of American bombing, the phasing down of the Cultural Revolution, and the emergence of Chou En-lai as the dominant figure in Chinese foreign policy—paved the way for China's emergence from isolation. In 1970 it established diplomatic relations with Canada even though the Canadians merely "took note" of Peking's claim to Taiwan rather than formally recognizing it. By the fall of 1971, Peking had established formal relations with about sixty nations. Since only America had the power to deter the Soviet Union from a preemptive strike at China's nuclear installations, an approach to Washington was a logical next move. Instead of encouraging the total removal of the American presence in the area, China began to see advantages in the continuance of American troop and naval deployments in Japan, Korea, and other forward positions in the Pacific. At the same time, it publicly urged NATO to stay strong and made clear its hope that America would continue to maintain its forces in Europe. . . .

Nixon Took Advantage of Good Timing

It was one of history's perverse whimsies that China began to unlock its doors to the rest of the world just when Nixon came to power, since Nixon's admiration for Communist China came late in life. As a young McCarthyite congressman, he had joined in denouncing the Truman Administration for "losing China." Even while campaigning for Vice President in 1952 he had charged that "China wouldn't have gone Communist—if the Truman Administration had backbone." Again, as recently as his 1960 campaign against John F. Kennedy, he had accused the Chinese Communists of seeking world domination.

Nevertheless, he must be given credit for conversion to a sounder view, when, in an article under his name in *Foreign Affairs* in October 1967, he observed that "any American policy toward Asia must come urgently to grips with the reality of China." Thus, before he assumed office, Nixon seems to have envisaged that China might be used as a counter to the Soviet Union. On March 1, 1969, he told [French leader] De Gaulle that he was determined to open a dialogue with Peking and that he foresaw the admission of Peking to the United Nations and the "normalization of relations." When De Gaulle came to Washington to attend Eisenhower's funeral, Nixon asked the general to convey the spirit of America's new policy to the Chinese—a message subsequently carried out through Etienne M. Manac'h, the French ambassador to Peking.

During 1969 the United States gave a series of small signals to China. The passports of scholars, journalists, and students were automatically validated on a reciprocal basis. United States naval patrols were suspended in the Taiwan Straits and nuclear weapons were removed from Okinawa. United States tourists were allowed to purchase up to one hundred dollars' worth of Chinese goods, which had been totally banned since 1950.

For several years the United States had been carrying on discussions with the Chinese through the ambassadors of the two countries in Warsaw, but these had been suspended in January 1968. When, in the fall of 1969, there was an indication through third nation channels that the Chinese might be interested in resuming these talks, Washington responded encouragingly. After proposing that the talks be moved to Peking, the Chinese gave positive signals to the United States, including an invitation to the American journalist Edgar Snow to stand next to Mao on China's national day. While the President was sending messages to Peking indicating that he wished to know whether or not "he or his representative would be received," Snow quoted Mao as saying, in December 1970, that the Chinese "were discussing whether Nixon might be permitted to come" to China. Finally, in the spring of 1971 a message was sent through the Pakistani ambassador inviting "an American envoy" to visit Peking, suggesting either Secretary of State Rogers or Kissinger.

The President kept all of this tightly secret, which, no doubt, disappointed the Chinese, whose principal purpose in opening the door to the United States was to make it unmistakable to the Soviet Union that they had a friend in Washington. From the Chinese point of view the louder and more blatant the American show of interest, the better. Thus, it was not the inscrutable Orientals but the traditionally open Americans who insisted on smothering the whole enterprise with a Béarnaise sauce of intrigue and mystery.

A Secret Trip to China

Kissinger's Pakistan caper set the tone for what was to follow. Flying to Islamabad, ostensibly for discussions with President Yahya Khan, he secluded himself, on the excuse of a "slight indisposition"—translated by the American press as "Delhi belly," which did not speak tactfully for the cuisine of the subcontinent. Actually, of course, he had been whisked off to Peking.

A great nation can obviously not enlist the complicity of a poor nation in a diplomatic melodrama without paying for it, and the United States later picked up the check

From *Herblock's State of the Union* (Simon & Schuster, 1972). Used with permission.

by siding with Pakistan against India in the Bangladesh affair. But, for the moment, the conspiratorial atmosphere of the enterprise placed the Secretary of the Pakistan Ministry of Foreign Affairs, Sultan Mohammed Khan, in an awkward position. Charged with handling the details of the trip, he had difficulty explaining to the Chinese why such clandestine arrangements were necessary. All be could think of to tell them was that the American Government was hard pressed by the "China lobby" and so did not yet dare let it be known that it was talking to Peking—a concept difficult to express in a foreign language.

To be fair, one could argue that the White House might wish to test the depth of the Chinese response before disclosing the preliminary talks. Yet that does not explain why, on Kissinger's return to Washington, the United States did not undertake full consultations with our allies, including Japan, which had the greatest interest at stake, before we announced such a flamboyant venture as the President's projected trip. In fact, we kept Tokyo in the dark until less than an hour before Nixon went on the air, when Secretary Rogers telephoned Japanese Ambassador Ushiba along with other ambassadors in Washington. The Administration's explanation, of course, was that consultation would have increased the chance of a leak. But was that important? No leak could have created anything like the breakage resulting from our neglect of consultation.

Not only was secrecy positively harmful but, for reasons I shall point out later, the President's visit itself was a mistake. The negotiation of a new relationship with China was ideally suited for emissary diplomacy, and in Henry Kissinger the President had available the ideal envoy. Not only had he thought deeply about world power relationships, but he knew the President's own thinking on foreign policy, since he was largely instrumental in shaping it.

Nixon Visited China as a Public Relations Move

The heart of the matter is that Nixon insisted on secrecy, neglected consultation, caught the country off balance with a surprise announcement, and cast the whole diplomatic venture in the framework of a summit visit purely for his own domestic purposes. Otherwise, there is no explanation for the script or for the failure to consult—a rejection of the normal courtesy any nation would expect from its close ally.

But a premature disclosure might detract from the domestic political benefit of a dramatic announcement; and he wished to milk all the emotion possible from the shock effect of what he proudly described as "the biggest surprise in history." The announcement of the President's trip and the trip itself—as distinct from the political decision to resume communications through Kissinger's visit—were a stratagem of domestic politics, and very little more than that.

That the stratagem proved effective for the intended purpose is undeniable. Without doubt it contributed heavily to Nixon's electoral victory of 1972; and in the dark summer of 1974 he constantly put it forward to offset his manifold delinquencies. But to argue, as many have, that the President had to visit China personally in order to persuade a reluctant America to accept a new China policy insults the good sense of the American people. Although there are, no doubt, situations in which diplomatic initiatives must be tailored primarily for domestic opinion, this was not one of them; nor do I believe that President Nixon thought it was. What he saw in the surprise announcement and the glamour of his visit was a chance to bedazzle and excite the country—to give the American people, in other words, the modern equivalent of a Roman circus; for, if it were no longer acceptable to feed Christians to the lions in a well-packed arena, one could still profit politically by offering color and excitement to the American voter. . . .

Like so many of Nixon's "great initiatives," the trip to China was an overblown episode that lacked either a careful follow-up or a conceptual positioning within a coherent body of policy. Had he taken account of our larger interests, he would, of course, have kept our allies informed. Approached at the right time, the Japanese Government would have welcomed the American move, rather than regarding it as a catastrophe. Had he sent an envoy to Peking instead of going himself, the position of China would not have been distorted in the appraisal of the world, nor would America have humiliated itself in the eyes of Asian critics by sending its President to the Court of the Middle Kingdom—an act which, translated into Western terms, held some of the overtones of Canossa.

Only domestic politics were effectively served. Had the President not gone to Peking, he would have probably never received such an overwhelming vote in the 1972 election, but, in the light of all that subsequently happened, would that have been so unfortunate? In fact, should we not learn one solemn lesson from the whole Chinese adventure? To design a diplomatic initiative primarily for its impact on domestic voters is a thoroughly bad idea.

THE WATERGATE
SCANDAL AND
THE END
OF NIXON'S
PRESIDENCY

NIXON USED THE PRESIDENCY TO EXERCISE PERSONAL POWER

ARTHUR G. NEAL

In this selection from his book *National Trauma and Collective Memory*, Arthur G. Neal claims that Nixon felt that the presidency provided him with a mandate to act freely, not only in the nation's interest but in his own. This attitude led Nixon to do all he could to cover up the Watergate Scandal, even paying hush money, hiding information, and exerting influence on officials involved in the investigations. An intense political warrior, Nixon regarded these illegal procedures as normal political tactics. But these tactics, and Nixon's guilt, began to grow apparent with the testimony of John Dean, a former member of Nixon's White House staff, before the Senate Watergate Committee.

Neal, a professor of sociology at Bowling Green State University, asserts that Nixon's abuses of his authority were a threat to the American political system, and that Nixon's resignation was probably the proper end to the scandal.

C RIMINALITY IS USUALLY ASSOCIATED WITH STREET CRIMES in the thinking of most Americans. The notion that the president of the United States was "a criminal" could not be readily comprehended by most Americans. Elements of both belief and disbelief blended in public perceptions. After all, Nixon's campaign had drawn upon the latent fears of Americans about potential criminal victimization through burglary, robbery, and other street crimes. The notion that the man who had waged a "law-and-order" campaign may himself be a criminal was shocking.

The Watergate affair was characterized by a gradual development and a slow beginning. Newspaper reports in June 1972 indicated that burglars had been caught breaking into the Democratic Headquarters that was located in the Watergate apartment-office complex in Washington, D.C. There was nothing unusually noteworthy about this. On a daily basis, newspapers are filled with such stories about minor offenses. Why anyone would want to break into the Democratic Headquarters and what they expected to accomplish were initially questions of only minor concern. . . .

The plot thickened during the subsequent trial and conviction of the men who had been caught in the burglary, when it was revealed that several of the men had served with the CIA and the FBI. The skills these men exhibited for engaging in criminal activities, such as unlawful entry and wiretapping, were not skills that had been learned casually or accidentally; they were as refined and elaborate as those of the men who engaged in the covert activities of our national security system. What were the motives of these men? Why did they do it? Who were they working for? Whose orders were being followed? In effect, suspicions developed that the Watergate break-in represented only the tip of an iceberg. Much more had to be involved. . . .

Nixon's War on His Political Enemies

In the thinking of Richard Nixon and his associates, the metaphor of "war" had been applied to the political campaign. The domestic "enemies" in the war consisted of all those opposed to Nixon's leadership or his policies. In the White House, an elaborate plan was devised for dealing with those whose names made the "enemies list." Men from the CIA and Nixon's immediate circle of advisers elaborated strategies for conducting covert operations, labeled as "dirty tricks." The plans included infiltrating the headquarters of each of the Democratic contenders, tapping their phones, stealing their stationery, forging signatures, and making photocopies of their written documents. Further plans included the use of the IRS for harassment and leaking information to the press that would discredit specific individuals, including unwarranted allegations about drunk driving and sexual misconduct.

The domestic foes included not only leaders of the political opposition, but also employees of the government who leaked information to the press about questionable government operations. Foremost among these was Daniel Ellsberg who "leaked" the Pentagon Papers to the *New York Times*. The Pentagon Papers revealed that many forms of deception and misrepresentation had been employed both by military and political officials to cover up blunders during the Vietnam War. President Nixon was outraged. Loyalty to his administration was seen as a primary responsibility by all government employees. Anything that would reflect negatively upon government policies was seen as subversive. Accordingly, a unit designated as "the plumbers" was created to prevent the leak of information to the press about government operations. Special efforts were made to embarrass and discredit Ellsberg; for example, his psychiatrist's office was broken into to uncover information about him that would be personally damaging.

Several critical events unfolded to establish links between the White House and the Watergate burglary. The first came with an announcement from Judge John J. Sirica that he had received a letter from James McCord, one of the men convicted of the Watergate break-in. McCord's letter indicated that the defendants had been paid to maintain their silence, that perjury had been committed, and that numerous participants in the episode had not yet been identified. Before the case ran its course, McCord and several others expressed concern about becoming scapegoats in efforts to conceal the involvement of top government officials. Serious crimes had been detected, and now someone would have to pay the price by becoming "the sacrificial lamb."

Successful leaders frequently are able to remain aloof from the unsavory work that is required in politics. The dirty work may be delegated to subordinates who are less visible and thus able to work in an underhanded way without being detected. While denying any White House involvement in the Watergate affair, the president attempted to use the CIA to circumvent an investigation by the FBI that was initiated by the federal judiciary. In effect, he was using one agency of the government to prevent another agency from doing its job. Such an attempt at the obstruction of justice suggested desperate efforts at concealment and cover-up. Eventually, it was Nixon's persistence in concealment and cover-up that resulted in the charge of obstruction of justice in the articles of impeachment.

The Case Against the President

After the evidence became clear that members of the White House staff were involved in attempts to cover up the Watergate affair, the Senate initiated its own investigation. Public opinion polls were indicating a rapid erosion of public trust in Nixon's leadership. In televised hearings, a member of the White House staff, John Dean, had been granted immunity to tell the Senate Watergate Committee what he knew about the cover-up. In a lengthy prepared statement, Dean testified that both the president and his aides had participated in attempts to stonewall the Watergate investigation. As Dean's testimony unfolded, the nation responded with astonishment. Both those who voted for Nixon and those who voted against him felt betrayed.

Divided opinion was reflected in the interpersonal debates that took place throughout the country. Stalwart supporters of Nixon could not believe the accusations that were made against him. Americans have the freedom to criticize the president of the United States in any way they wish, but the level of discourse was seen by some as sinking to new levels. Some of the Republicans on the Senate Watergate Committee took extreme measures to discredit Dean's testimony. Each question and each answer was closely monitored within an adversarial context. Dean was a ready-made target as the first high-ranking official to reveal his own illegal activities and those of other members of the White House staff. There was a great deal of uneasiness both within the government and within the general public. The substantive issues on Nixon's complicity were far from being settled.

Determining what the president knew and when he knew it were foremost in the minds of many people. Dean's allegations stood in sharp contrast to Nixon's persistent denials. The president had previously announced publicly that an investigation from his office indicated that no member of the White House staff was involved. Whom should one believe, Dean or Nixon? An answer came through the testimony of Alexander Butterfield, a former White House aide. Butterfield revealed that a sophisticated recording system had been installed in the White House early in 1971 for recording all conversations and phone calls. Certainly, the recording of all conversations in the White House would indicate one way or the other whether or not the president was involved. The tapes potentially contained the "smoking gun" for implicating the president.

Both the special prosecutor, Archibald Cox, and the Senate Watergate Committee issued a subpoena for the White House tapes. It was the first time a subpoena had been issued to the president of the United States since the administration of Thomas Jefferson. Nixon refused to comply on the grounds of "executive privilege." He maintained that the tapes were confidential and the exclusive property of the president. When Cox insisted, Nixon ordered Attorney General Eliot Richardson to fire him. The refusal of Richardson to do so resulted in what came to be called the "Saturday-night massacre." Nixon removed from office both Richardson and his deputy William Ruckelshaus, who also had refused to fire Cox. Solicitor General Robert Bork carried out Nixon's order by firing Cox and sealing the records in the special prosecutor's office. The outrage at this abuse of power resulted in further demands that Nixon release the tapes and that a new Watergate prosecutor be appointed.

As the pressure for the release of the tapes mounted, the impasse was resolved by placing the case before the Supreme Court. As a last-ditch effort, Nixon was convinced that the court would rule in favor of the principle of "executive privilege." The court did not. In a unanimous decision, the court ruled that Nixon must turn over the tapes as requested by the special Watergate prosecutor and by the Senate committee. Nixon responded by agreeing to release a transcript of the tapes, with only irrelevancies deleted, but not the tapes themselves. The proposal of releasing only an edited transcript was rejected by the judiciary. Nothing short of a release of the tapes themselves would be acceptable. Even the president of the United States must comply with an order issued by the Supreme Court.

When the tapes were finally released, eighteen minutes of a conversation, taped shortly after the Watergate burglary, had been erased. However, the tapes clearly indicated that the president had knowledge of the attempted cover-up from the very beginning and had participated in it. The nation was shocked at the vulgarity of the conversations among those in the inner circle at the White House and by what they were talking about. Clearly those at the center of power saw themselves as standing above the law as they planned clandestine operations against individuals and against other agencies of the government. The evidence was now clear that Nixon had participated in an obstruction of justice and thus had violated his oath of office. . . .

Abuses of Power Were a Threat to the American System

Those having a serious interest in American politics quickly saw a threat to the American system of government. The crimes of the Nixon administration had been exposed, and if they were ignored, all future presidents could consider themselves free to arbitrarily abuse the power that was inherent in the office. A failure to act when action was necessary would set a precedent for transforming the American system of government. Either the president would have to resign or he would have to be impeached and forcefully removed from office.

The move to impeach a president is a serious undertaking. Prior to the impeachment proceedings against Nixon, only one other attempt had been made to impeach a president in the history of the nation. In 1868, impeachment proceedings were brought against President Andrew Johnson. Historians now agree that the charges brought against Johnson were politically motivated and based on shameful and unwarranted allegations. Andrew Johnson had been seen as overly conciliatory in his attitudes toward the South and in his plans for reconstruction following the carnage of the Civil War. Several members of the House Judiciary Committee were fearful that history was about to repeat itself. The charges brought against Nixon seemed unbelievable and lacking in credibility. Many believed the enemies of Richard Nixon were out to get him.

Following the release of the tapes, support for the president eroded rapidly, even among many who previously had been loyal to him. Calls for his resignation were issued by newspapers, by Republican leaders in the Senate, and by influential people throughout the country. The trauma to the nation was of sufficient severity that prolonging the agony seemed unnecessary. All members of the House Judiciary Committee were now in favor of impeachment. Prior indecision evaporated as the high drama recorded in the White House tapes was revealed. Very few people in Congress, in the federal judiciary, or in the public at large desired to have Nixon remain in office. Consensus had now been reached that either Nixon would resign or be impeached and convicted of the crimes he had committed. The reasonable options available to the president were diminishing very rapidly.

Full impeachment proceedings in the House and subsequent trial and conviction in the Senate would be a long, drawn-out affair that very few, if anyone, really wanted. The time had come to abandon ship, so to speak, and only a small number of stalwarts were willing to further support the president. The two-thirds vote in the Senate that was needed for his conviction now seemed a certainty. Yet, Nixon tenaciously held on to the office. After all, he had been duly elected as president of the United States, and in his view, his actions were fully in the best interests of the nation.

There was concern about what Nixon might actually do out of a sense of desperation. As president, he was the commander-in-chief of the armed forces and had final control over the use of nuclear weapons. Out of a concern from what might happen under the circumstances, Defense Secretary James Schlesinger issued a directive to all military commanders that no direct order from the White House would be carried out without his counter-signature. The dangers inherent in the situation seemed to warrant such precautions.

The personal despair and anguish of Nixon was preventing him from attending to the affairs of state. With some degree of uneasiness, the president's assistant Alexander Haig had for some time been doing most of the routine work that was needed for the continuity of the office. There was also a concern among some of those close to the president that he might commit suicide. Personal appeals were cautiously made to Nixon for him to cut his losses and to resign with dignity. It was no longer in his own best interest or in the best interest of the nation for him to continue.

On August 8, 1974, the nation encountered one of the more emotional moments in its history when the thirty-seventh president of the United States went on television and announced to the world, "I shall resign the presidency effective at noon tomorrow." The drama of his resignation has often been described as having the ingredients of a Greek tragedy. The agony of recent events was rapidly coming to a close. The following day, the nation watched as Nixon gave his farewell to the White House staff and boarded a military helicopter for his move into exile. With mixed emotions, the nation sighed with relief. . . .

Nixon Wanted to Exert Personal Power

For Nixon the prize of the political game was personal power and what he personally saw as being in the best interests of the country. Regardless of the scandals of Watergate and his forced resignation, Nixon apparently believed that history would look favorably upon his administration. In his view, it is the political accomplishments of the man that really matter, rather than the means he employed in attaining them. Those who stand in opposition to "national interests" have to be dealt with in a heavy-handed way. Civil liberties and due process must be suspended if they interfere with "national security" concerns.

The autobiographical writings of former presidents, in some way or another, address the issue of a differential between the experience "of power" and the experience "with power." Lyndon Johnson, for example, was a man who had a reputation for arm-twisting; however, he was not able to set the national agenda he wished to promote. The emerging issues that require the attention of the president are frequently not of his own choosing. Further, the personal power of the president is limited by the many constituencies that he has to confront and deal with in some way or another. Harry Truman wrote about the loneliness of the office that grows out of the monumental decisions that the president alone must make and for which he alone must accept responsibility. Presiding over a nation thus involves much more than the personal desires and wishes of the man who holds the office.

The special case of Richard Nixon was one in which he regarded his election as a personal mandate. The sense of power that accompanied the office was translated into a sense of personal invulnerability. He felt free to do whatever he wanted to do as long as it was concealed from the public. To avoid the loneliness described by Truman, he surrounded himself with like-minded individuals. A primary criterion for the selection of subordinates was total loyalty and dedication to his leadership. The ideology of "national interests" and "national security" was drawn upon to justify the use of unethical procedures.

Some believed the forced resignation of Nixon confirmed the integrity of the political process. All of the major branches of government played a key role in the removal of Nixon from office. There were men of integrity who chose to resign rather than carry out Nixon's orders, which were improperly given. Even the Nixon supporters within his own party came to feel betrayed and decided that nothing short of Nixon's resignation was acceptable. The abuse of power became an insult to the men and women of integrity who had devoted their lives to public service.

WATERGATE WAS THE PRODUCT OF NIXON'S INSECURITIES

ALONZO L. HAMBY

Richard Nixon had always felt himself to be a political outsider. He came from California, which was a state from which no president had previously been elected, and he was also born into a poor family. In addition, Nixon did not have an Ivy League education. He seemed to believe that the political establishment held those things against him.

According to Alonzo L. Hamby, from whose book *Liberalism and Its Challengers* the following selection is taken, Nixon's insecurities helped lead to the Watergate break-in and the subsequent cover-up. Hamby, a professor of history at Ohio State University, maintains that Nixon often reacted in a mean-spirited, amoral manner and created a negative atmosphere which inspired his aides to use questionable tactics such as bugging offices and hiding information. In the end, Nixon failed not only to control his aides but also to be honest to himself and the nation.

I N JUNE 1972, THE DISTRICT OF COLUMBIA POLICE TOOK into custody five burglars who had broken into the offices of the Democratic National Committee at the fashionable Watergate complex in Washington, apparently to plant a listening device. A trail of clues led incredibly from the perpetrators—three Cuban émigrés and two native-born Americans, all with CIA connections—to E. Howard

---

Hunt, an administration consultant who a dozen years earlier had helped plan the Bay of Pigs invasion, and to G. Gordon Liddy, a Republican campaign official. All seven men were indicted; the head of the Nixon campaign committee, the president's close friend, former Attorney General John Mitchell, denied prior knowledge but resigned all the same.

As the Watergate Seven awaited trial that fall, the Democrats attempted unsuccessfully to make an issue of the episode. The American electorate, apparently unwilling to face the prospect of a McGovern presidency, behaved almost as a willing conspirator in the increasingly dubious pretense that the break-in had been the work of a few overzealous underlings. In fact, Nixon himself had secretly allowed his top domestic aide, H. R. Haldeman, to dissuade the FBI from a serious investigation that would have demonstrated otherwise.

Watergate Summarized

Throughout 1973 and into 1974, the cover-up slowly came apart, partly because of pressure from a determined opposition, partly because Nixon and those around him displayed monumental ineptitude and inexplicable irresolution in dealing with a matter of political life and death. The events are well known: the conviction; the original Watergate burglars; the decision of their leader to implicate hitherto untouched administration figures; an investigation conducted by a special Senate committee headed by Sam Ervin of North Carolina; indictments of more administration figures; the resignations of FBI Director L. Patrick Gray and Attorney General Richard Kleindeinst; the appointment of Archibald Cox as special prosecutor; the discovery that the president had taped most of his confidential conversations; the inexorable push to make the tapes public; the Saturday Night Massacre firing of Cox and others in October, 1973; the conviction of various administration officials on charges such as perjury and obstruction of justice; continued pressure from a new special prosecutor Leon Jaworski; the issuance of some "sanitized" transcripts; court orders mandating full release of the tapes. Along the way, there also occurred the forced resignation of Vice-President Agnew under charges of taking illegal payoffs, an Internal Revenue Service assessment against the president for back taxes, and the revelation that some of the Watergate burglars bad been part of a White House "plumbers" unit that had engaged in other illegal activities. During the last week of July 1974, the House Judiciary Committee recommended impeachment. A few days later, Nixon was forced by his own angry lawyers to release the "smoking gun" transcript of June 23, 1972, proving conclusively that the president long had known about cover-up efforts. On August 8, 1974, he became the first chief executive in American history to resign from office.

As with any series of events played out on the level of epic drama, Watergate was utterly fascinating in itself—for its human interest, its complexity, and its alteration of the course of American history. Beyond the public view of powerful men parading from the Senate committee rooms to the courtrooms and thence to public disgrace, however, there remain compelling questions. How could Watergate have happened in the first place? And how could a trivial surreptitious entry about which a president almost certainly had no advance knowledge be allowed to become a national obsession for nearly a year and a half? And how could this obsession bring down a leader who had been elected by overwhelming majorities? The answers appear to reside within Richard Nixon—in his own insecure, meanspirited personality and the responses it aroused.

Nixon Played Political Hardball

The break-in occurred on the evening of June 17, a week and a half after George McGovern had won the California primary, locked up the Democratic nomination, and thereby assured Nixon of an easy victory in November. Manifestly, it was not required by the exigencies of a close campaign. Nor was it particularly mitigated by the fact that other administrations had engaged in political bugging and other dirty tricks. At bottom it was yet another reflection of Nixon's reflex combativeness and anything-goes approach to politics. Nixon, Agnew, and Mitchell had passed down to the third and fourth echelons an attitude that the opposition was illegitimate and that the political contest with them might reasonably have a dimension of secret warfare not unlike that waged by the CIA against its Soviet counterparts.

Nixon's team not only reciprocated the hatred of the Democrats but also acquired the vindictiveness and ruthless amorality that always had characterized their chief's approach to politics. Nixon recalls of Charles Colson, one of the central figures of the cover-up, "I had always valued his hard-ball instincts." It followed naturally enough that Colson sensed his leader's priorities. So also did many of the other operatives close to the president: H. R. Haldeman, John Ehrlichman, John Dean, and John Mitchell all demonstrated no qualms about the destruction of evidence, perjury, and hush money payments. *Their* subordinates imbibed the mood also.

Thus, the Watergate break-in seemed a plausible enough course of action. It was simply another battle, however poor the tactical conception, in a continuing war. A stern denunciation and a sincere effort to hunt out the culprits probably never seriously entered the mind of the president and those around him. Instead they instinctively moved to control the damage by initiating a cover-up; rather than remove themselves from the problem, they made themselves part of it.

Curiously, Nixon knew better. In one of his last meetings with John Dean, he recalled the fatal mistake of his old adversary, Alger Hiss: "That son of a bitch Hiss would be free today [sic] if he hadn't lied. If he had said, 'Yes I knew Chambers and as a young man I was involved with some Communist activities but I broke it off a number of years ago.' And Chambers would have dropped it. If you are going to lie, you go to jail for the lie rather than the crime. So believe me, don't ever lie." Strangely, he proved incapable of taking his own good advice.

Nixon's Many Enemies React

Nixon has argued, not altogether fallaciously, that bugging and other political "dirty tricks" had been practiced by both political parties and virtually every president since FDR. From his perspective, Watergate was still another cause, magnified beyond its actual importance, to be used by all those forces in American life that long had delighted in kicking Dick Nixon around. As the cover-up was in the early stages of its slow but inexorable collapse in March 1973, Nixon held a press conference. "The questioning kept returning to Watergate with a relentlessness, almost a passion, that I had seen before only in the most emotional days of the Vietnam war," he recalls. "For the first time I began to realize the dimensions of the problem we were facing with the media and with Congress regarding Watergate: *Vietnam had found its successor.*"

There was something to be said for this analysis; yet it was at most a slanted, woefully incomplete explanation. It was true enough that Nixon had long been detested by both the Democratic party and the adversary culture in American life and that he had a hate relationship with the majority of the journalists who covered him. What it does not explore is the question of why this was the case; other Republican leaders, Nelson Rockefeller the prime example, did not carry such burdens. Nixon's cut-and-slash attacks against liberal Democrats, the intelligentsia, and the press had inflicted scars beyond the norms of most political

The Watergate Break-in Was Unnecessary

Nixon's original chief-of-staff, H.R. Haldeman, wondered in his memoirs why the Watergate break-in took place.

Nixon had been through hell in his first four years in office. The Vietnam War had created almost unbearable pressures which caused him to order wiretaps, and activate the Plumbers in response to antiwar moves. But by June 1972, he was miraculously on top. His May 8, 1972, bombing of North Vietnam and mining of Haiphong Harbor had decisively stopped the North Vietnamese advance and caused their leaders to make their first serious move in four years toward peace. His diplomatic achievements with China and Russia had been enormously successful. His popularity was at an all-time high. And the Democratic candidates had been flattened by the McGovern steamroller, with the result that the party's weakest candidate was an odds-on favorite to win the nomination.

Nixon's own re-election was secure. Why then risk everything by sending burglars after political information in the Democratic National Committee Headquarters at a time when it wasn't needed? Especially as every professional politician in Washington (including Nixon and myself) knew that no political knowledge of any value could ever be found in party headquarters. The candidates' headquarters contained all the vital information. The Democratic National Committee, like its Republican counterpart, is little more than a ceremonial shell before the convention takes place.

H.R. Haldeman with Joseph DiMona, *The Ends of Power*. New York: Times Books, 1978.

combat. It was hardly surprising that the *Washington Post* should take up the issue of Watergate with special gusto against an administration that had publicly impugned its integrity and organized challenges to the renewal of its television licenses. And it was natural enough that many Democrats retained ugly memories of the fate of Jerry Voorhis and Helen Gahagan Douglas. Nixon's past, a past he had never repudiated, had made him the most vehemently hated man in American politics and left him peculiarly vulnerable.

Throughout 1973, one development after another, from the defection of John Dean to the desperate Saturday Night Massacre, destroyed Nixon's credibility. Even in their sanitized, "expletive deleted" state, the transcripts released in April 1974 made Nixon and his aides appear to be sleazy, foul-mouthed, amoral operators who thought only of public relations. They showed that the president had at least come close to sanctioning a cover-up. They demonstrated that no later than March 21, 1973, John Dean had informed Nixon of an ongoing situation that included perjury, obstruction of justice, and payment of blackmail by White House functionaries, and that the president had treated it all as a problem to be handled pragmatically rather than a series of crimes to be exposed. The transcripts contained numerous passages in which the president had anticipated the maximum use of federal power against the administration's enemies.

By this time, something else had emerged as an indicator of the moral atmosphere of the White House—the efforts of some of the people enmeshed in Watergate to save themselves by implicating others. John Dean, counsel to the president, an ambitious young man not overly burdened with scruples, had participated in the early stages of the cover-up with few qualms, but he began to worry when it became clear that the opposition would not let the issue die a natural death. He jumped ship when he perceived that the president was setting him up to take the rap. Dean's suspicions probably were well founded, and his testimony before the Ervin Committee, truthful if a bit self-serving, was crucial in destroying the president whom he had served.

Dean's sense of betrayal seems to have been felt by numerous individuals, ranging from Howard Hunt, who engaged in what amounted to blackmail demands for money and clemency, to Haldeman and Ehrlichman, who felt the ground collapse under their feet when their chief fired them under pressure and ultimately refused to grant them a presidential pardon before leaving office himself. It was a measure of Nixon's confidence in his own aides that, by his own admission, he worried for months that John Dean might have surreptitiously taped some of their Watergate-related conversations.

The President Had Chances to Save Himself

Had Nixon acted more decisively at two critical points, he could have survived Watergate. His reputation would have been damaged, but he still could have functioned as chief executive. The first critical point came a few days after the break-in, when he could have come down against a cover-up and disowned any aide guilty of complicity in a shabby little crime. He might have done the same thing with more difficulty after the election. The second critical point came with the public discovery of the president's taping system. Only a group of audio tapes over which the president possessed full authority could confirm the charges brought against him. Their destruction would have made his removal from office almost impossible. Nixon's refusal to act doomed him. His inability to make the moves necessary to save himself strikes one as not simply the product of mistaken calculation but of deep-seated insecurity and self-destructiveness.

Why didn't he act? Nixon himself has faced this question with some openness, and much of what he says deserves to be taken at face value.

He probably was concerned, as he has claimed, with the fate of his close friends and associates, Mitchell, Haldeman, and Ehrlichman, whom he surely knew beyond a doubt to be involved in obstruction of justice. To let them down and face their rejection would have been an unpleasant prospect for a stronger man. To an individual of Nixon's insecurity, it was a nearly unendurable possibility. Characteristically, he attempted to transmute his reluctance to face the facts into a virtue, a nonpartisan virtue. "Whatever we say about old Harry Truman," he told John Ehrlichman at a point when Ehrlichman was desperately in need of reassurance, "while it hurt him, a lot of people admired the old bastard for standing by people who were guilty as hell, and, damn it, I am that kind of person. I am not one who is going to say, look, while this guy is under attack, I drop him."

Aside from exaggerating Truman's tolerance of criminal behavior, Nixon had also evaded the question of his responsibility as the nation's chief executive. As Henry Petersen, the federal prosecutor in charge of the Watergate investigation at that time, told Nixon, his reluctance to fire Haldeman and Ehrlichman might speak well for him as a man but poorly for him as a president. Two weeks later, events forced him to accept their resignations all the same, leaving them angry and disillusioned. Later, Nixon would recall the old British maxim that a successful prime minister had to be a good butcher. With self-pity and some hope of exculpation, he would declare that he had not been a good butcher. True enough; and, like most acts of bad butchery, his irresolute behavior had made a situation worse. Ultimately, what was at issue was the national interest, the duties of the presidency, and the preservation of the office itself; it was these Nixon butchered devastatingly.

Nixon also has addressed the problem of why he failed

to destroy the tapes. Until very late in the game, the tapes were an unknown quantity, recorded, stored, and never reviewed. After their existence became known, after the Ervin Committee had subpoenaed them and the issue had become a matter for the courts, it became positively dangerous for White House staff members to listen to them. Knowledge of the tapes entangled one in a steadily growing web; it might entail embarrassing appearances before congressional committees or courts of law and expensive legal representation. Not knowing precisely what was on the tapes, Nixon probably did not realize how damaging they were. He has written that he believed they would exonerate him rather than convict him!

Still, it is hard to imagine that he ever really believed that they could be more helpful than harmful. It is equally difficult to assume that he thought that over the long haul be could withstand what was certain to be an intense public campaign for their release. One is driven to wonder whether Nixon preserved the tapes precisely because he knew he had done wrong and possessed some need to be punished.

A Pattern of Insecure Behavior

Like many individuals who receive and internalize a set of rigid behavioral standards in their youth, Nixon had departed from values that had been deeply instilled in him in order to get ahead in the hard adult world; yet, far from abandoning those values, he proclaimed them at every opportunity and sought to make himself their personification. The contrast between his behavior and his rhetoric might appear a simple case of conscious hypocrisy, but in all probability it was a guilt-inducing situation that plagued him constantly.

Throughout Nixon's account of Watergate and many other episodes in his career, one finds a defensive, self-pitying tone that must indicate an attempt to cope with intimations of guilt. Envisioning his life as that of a man who moves from one extreme situation (crisis) to another, he places himself in settings that require more than ordinary morality. Constantly employing *tuquoque* argumentation [the idea that whatever one does is justified if others have done it before], he asserts that his behavior is no different from that of others in the real world, that the indulgence of his opponents in various dirty tricks requires him to do the same sort of thing. Invariably depicting himself as a man set upon by implacable enemies, he attempts to shift the reader's attention from his motivation to that of those who are out to get him. The difficulty of managing this burden may well be the ultimate explanation of Nixon's politically suicidal behavior during the last year and a half of his administration. In his forced resignation from office, he at last experienced the judgment he probably had come to feel he deserved.

Tragically, that judgment extended not just to the man but to the political and diplomatic principles with which he had attempted to identify himself and, finally, to the office of the presidency as it had evolved by the end of the sixties. Nixon's major domestic and foreign policies were flawed, to be sure, and scarcely as successful as his defenders would have us believe. Nonetheless, they represented interesting, important efforts to adjust American life and American diplomacy to new realities. At his best, Nixon the domestic policy maker attempted to come to grips with problems that his liberal opponents had brought into being and had consistently dodged. Nixon the diplomatist engaged in an earnest and, for the most part, constructive effort to adjust U.S. foreign policy to an increasingly difficult world in which the nation no longer could assume either military or economic preeminence. A better man with fewer psychological burdens and more substantial qualities of leadership might have avoided many of the negative aspects of the Nixon presidency and won recognition as an above-average president. Nixon achieved only a personal disaster. Worse, he left the presidency itself an object of suspicion and scorn, awaiting a new Roosevelt or Eisenhower to restore its standing and provide a demoralized public with a sense of movement and purpose that could come only from the occupant of the White House.

The Importance of
Watergate Has Been
Exaggerated

Maurice H. Stans

Richard Nixon was a man of great political experience and skill who was elected president at a very difficult time in the nation's history. After his election in 1968, he was asked not only to address a number of domestic problems, but also to end the war in Vietnam and help maintain peace among the superpowers. In doing so, he was continually frustrated by opposition from Congress and the media. In addition, Nixon claimed that he was always the victim of information leaks. He thought those leaks greatly hampered his ability to make decisions.

Maurice Stans, in this selection from his book *The Terrors of Justice: The Untold Side of Watergate*, argues that Nixon's actions during Watergate were understandable. Stans, secretary of commerce in Nixon's cabinet, contends that the original break-in was simply a misguided effort by members of a team of "plumbers" Nixon's staff had assembled to stop information leaks. In any case, Stans claims, earlier presidents were also guilty. They had behaved badly and, when they believed it was necessary, misused their presidential authority.

WHEN NIXON RAN FOR THE PRESIDENCY IN 1968 HE WAS probably the best trained man the country had ever found for the job. He had been Vice President for two full terms, even a sort of Acting President during a severe

Excerpted from *The Terrors of Justice: The Untold Side of Watergate*, by Maurice H. Stans (New York: Everest House, 1978). Copyright ©1978 by Maurice H. Stans. Reprinted by permission of the Estate of Maurice H. Stans.

illness of Dwight Eisenhower. He had been in the tough world of business for eight years, with an opportunity realized by few high-level politicians and only a few previous Presidents to see at first hand how the nation's productive wheels turn.

There can be no doubt that in all these experiences a man of his analytical capacity would be accumulating ideas as to what the country needed for its long-term future, and what the world of nations needed. These ideas could easily be translated into what he would do if he were President—perhaps not as a program in numbered paragraphs but as a partly conscious, partly subconscious catalog of plans that could be drawn upon. There is no doubt in my mind that on January 20, 1969, as he took the oath of office, Richard Nixon had such a concept of his forthcoming job, and that he wanted through the powers of his office to improve life in the country and in the world.

He knew it would be difficult. His Republican party was in the minority in both houses of the Congress, which meant that he could expect an item-by-item struggle to get legislation enacted. That is exactly what occurred. Some of his proposals were badly abused, some not enacted at all, some twisted into shapes he could not accept. It was a running fight, and he geared up to cope with it as best he could. Meanwhile, he was confronted from the outset with the bane of Presidents, unauthorized news leaks; his plans were often telegraphed ahead to the opposition and even the minor performance gaps of his administration were public property, bitingly criticized....

Nixon Uses the "Plumbers" to Stop Leaks

Nixon tried to cope with the leaks, first through a series of national security wiretaps, and then by allowing his staff to set up a so-called "plumbers" group. The theft and release to the press of the Pentagon papers in 1971 by Daniel Ellsberg sent his blood pressure to the ceiling, and caused him to demand that somehow, some way, something be done to punish Ellsberg and set an example. His aides took it from there and performed disastrously.

Digging hard to locate leaks of information that ought to be privileged, if done within the proprieties of the law, is one thing and is understandable; using governmental power in illegal actions that abort due process is another and cannot be condoned. The nocturnal invasion of the office of Ellsberg's psychiatrist did more than result in Ellsberg going free for an offense for which he probably should have been convicted; when it became known, it disturbed a large body of public opinion because it showed a disregard for the orderly institutional and legal ways of the country. More than anything these actions of his subordinates hurt Nixon severely when they came to light. . . .

Within this environment, one of the "plumbers" group, Gordon Liddy, apparently proposed to a campaign official, Jeb Magruder, that some benefit might be gained if the moves of the political opposition could be anticipated, perhaps by bugging their phones or reading their files or putting informers into their organization. Or possibly it was the other way, Magruder to Liddy. Equivalent tactics had been used before, by both parties. That was presumably the genesis of Watergate. That is how a plot as absurd and as petty and as fruitless as the Watergate burglary came to happen.

The President Knew Nothing About the Watergate Break-in

Nixon was not a party to the Watergate break-in. That has been established, especially by the White House tapes beginning in June 1972, which showed his initial consternation at learning about it. Why then did he apparently allow himself to be involved, first passively and then actively, in the coverup? Why did he not insist on immediate full disclosure in June 1972? Was his knee-jerk approval of the coverup a case of his being instinctively evil or instinctively protective?

Only Richard Nixon can answer those questions and it is possible that even he, in retrospect, may not be sure of the answers, since some of the early decisions were so lightly considered. Writers will speculate about them endlessly, as they have, with little or no authority for their conclusions about what went on in the man's mind. The preponderance of present judgment among Americans seems to be that, since he is evil, given to profanity and some obscenity, his motivation was deliberately criminal. With no less right to conjecture, it is possible to believe that his motivation was wholly patriotic, and within that goal little thought was given to alternatives or eventualities. Nixon wanted to protect his close aides from the consequences of their escapades; he wanted to protect his campaign from being harmed; he wanted to protect his administration from repeated censure; and above all he wanted to protect his opportunity to pursue his goals for the nation.

I cannot be sure how calculatingly he made that decision; it may have been wholly casual, or it may have been made with benefit of some deliberation. But I think a case can be made for his believing that, in preventing the facts of Watergate from being known, and with it the "plumbers" operation, he was doing a necessary service to his country. He may have been trying to insure that his positive programs for the nation would have the greatest possible chance for success, which would not be likely if the mandate he hoped to obtain and did obtain on November 7 was severely marred, or even lost, by disclosures of impropriety in his organization. In this manner he could reason that, since he was not covering acts of his own, the national benefits of the coverup far outweighed the normal objections of conscience.

Just as some of his top associates thought in the case of the "plumbers" that a little bit of illegality was permissible to counter the potential damage to national security caused by persistent and sometimes illegal leaks, so could he have concluded that some drastic action was necessary to prevent his objectives for the nation from being undermined. That line of thought would not be unlikely in a man so totally dedicated to his mission and so sure of his course. He grabbed at the straws offered by his key subordinates, trusted them, cussed out all concerned, and returned to his desk.

The President Grows Frustrated

Then when the propped-up structure began to collapse, as McCord, Dean, and the other culprits one by one began to walk out from under, the frustration at the top was unbearable. The wild thrashing around for something to grab onto for survival generated brusque profanity and light obscenity on the inside, and mistruths and equivocation on the outside. The oppressive struggle with a problem that wouldn't be solved drove him to desperation and his greatest mistakes, because then he lost touch with reality and no longer could cope. Suddenly it was a hopeless coverup that stumbled on erratically until it eventually fell apart in all directions. Desperate firings and hirings, speeches, press conferences, and counter-posed leaks served little purpose to stem the tide once the dam had broken. The President had no choice but to abdicate. He had lost everything.

None of this excuses the actions, but it does rationalize them. However one divides the unfulfilled responsibility among those in the play, there still remains the necessity to balance out the failings of Richard Nixon in this one series of events against his worthy deeds as a lifetime public servant.

What about the tapes which so harshly seem to indict him in his own words? The expletives, I believe, should be dismissed, not because they are in any sense proper, but because they can be condoned under the pressures of the office. Dwight Eisenhower could be as caustically profane as Richard Nixon; I heard him many times. Lyndon Johnson was noted for vulgar expressions. I doubt that Harry Truman or John Kennedy were much more pious under the stress of tough decisions or unnerving frustrations.

Only a tiny fraction of the tapes has been made public. Who knows what genius or generosity by Nixon may be contained in those not revealed? Again, time and events may bring about a more favorable balance of evidence.

Why was there a taping system at all? On this I have no difficulty in accepting his own reply. He wanted the tapes to preserve a record of history in the making. Being distrustful of the daily media and their impact on the writing of history, he wanted incontrovertible first-hand evidence to back his own accounts of how events were handled in his administration. He was not the first President to use this device for that purpose, but he did it on a larger scale. Ironically, their worst parts turned the public against him, without anyone knowing what the best parts might have recorded. . . .

Watergate Must Be Placed in the Context of the Times

It is easy now to forget the political and social climate which Nixon inherited and which he ultimately turned around in his first term. The unpopular Vietnam war, which had accelerated during the Johnson Administration to a point at which more than a half million men were endangered in that small, distant country, with deaths of more than 300 a week and thousands injured, had produced widespread disaffection. The youth of the country were, understandably, in revolt against the whole adventure. Political differences were wide—between a Goldwater calling for all-out victory and a McGovern demanding instant withdrawal. To many, the nation's pride rode on the outcome. To others, a social revolution required abandonment of many traditional values, including patriotism.

Flags were burned in protest; draft cards were publicly torn up. Violence begot violence, and public attention exalted leaders of violence. It was a distressing time in the nation's life—one of great tension and polarization, of angry demonstration and vicious name calling, and of talk about overthrowing the government. Worse, it was a period in which judges and policemen were being murdered, ordinary citizens kidnapped and highjacked, and life was insecure; when public buildings, even the United States Capitol, were being bombed, and riots were gutting parts of our cities. It was an age of revolution, guerrillas, and terrorism.

This was a time to try the soul and the capacity of any President, and it was Nixon's misfortune that when he took office he had to walk directly into the limelight with the task of extricating the nation, with some semblance of honor, from the Vietnam conflict and quiet the strident forces in the nation. It is understandable that, in the course of that mission, he would think it necessary to use strong tactics against those he considered to be the leaders of the subversion and the contributors to its force. . . .

It seems true now that Nixon did no worse than two or three of his predecessors in using this kind of power to protect the country, safeguard his administration, or harass his enemies. However, precedent does not justify wrongdoing. While the precedents set by others in office before him may not excuse some of Nixon's apparent misuse of investigative agencies, they certainly do make his actions easier to comprehend, and they do raise the question of whether he was not grossly over-maligned and over-punished for them. In my heart, I cannot seriously fault Nixon on this count.

The Watergate Break-In Was Misunderstood

Jonathan Aitken

Richard Nixon placed a great deal of faith in his aides. They included Chief of Staff H.R. Haldeman, Domestic Adviser John Ehrlichman, Attorney General John Mitchell, and White House Counsel John Dean. In return for this faith, Nixon expected loyalty and obedience. Perhaps following Nixon's example, these aides sometimes used dubious tactics in order to achieve their political goals or to serve their president—the Watergate break-in itself was the work of aides, rather than Nixon himself.

In his biography of Nixon, from which this selection is taken, Jonathan Aitken makes the case that the Watergate break-in was misunderstood from the beginning. Instead of an attempt to bug the offices of Lawrence O'Brien, chairman of the Democratic National Committee, the break-in was part of John Dean's long-term plan to discredit Democratic officials. Dean was looking for links, Aitken asserts, between low-level Democratic Party employees and a prostitution ring in Washington, D.C. Both in the break-in and in the subsequent cover-up, Dean manipulated and lied to all involved. Consequently, argues Aitken, Dean should be held responsible for Watergate rather than Nixon. Nixon's "fatal error" was failing to control Dean, Aitken holds, and history may judge his involvement in Watergate in a more positive light. Aitken was a member of the British Parliament from 1974 to 1997, and has also served as both the minister of defense and of the treasury.

Excerpted from *Nixon: A Life*, by Jonathan Aitken. Copyright ©1993 by Henry Regnery Publishing. All rights reserved. Reprinted by special permission of Regnery Publishing, Inc., Washington, D.C.

W ATERGATE WAS A SHAKESPEAREAN TRAGEDY FOR Richard Nixon. According to most Washington reviewers, he was the actor who played all the most villainous parts: motivator of the break-in; architect of the cover-up; betrayer of the constitution; tape-wiper extraordinary; venal tax dodger; obscenitor most foul; and criminal-in-chief. Such characterisations brought comfort to America's liberal establishment and joy to its journalists. Their righteous certainty that Nixon got what he deserved has, until recently, been the authorised version of history.

Challenging this version is an uphill struggle, for the President's role in this self-inflicted crisis was undoubtedly an ignoble one. Even the most generous explanations for his conduct do not bring him exculpation. In his frenzied efforts to fight his way out of the quicksand of Watergate, Nixon made himself guilty of many 'crimes'— among them deceit, negligence, bad judgement, mendacity, amorality, concealment, and a disastrous reluctance to face up to uncomfortable personal confrontations with the individuals who were creating the worst problems. But were these 'crimes' simply personal and political acts of folly or did they become real criminal actions so serious in nature that Nixon deserved to be ejected in disgrace from the Presidency of the United States? Did the punishment fit the 'crime'? Did Congress handle the crisis in the best interests of the United States? Was the media's judgement on Watergate a fair one? So strong has been the tide of anti-Nixon sentiment that such questions have rarely been asked, let alone answered. Yet as the twentieth anniversary of Watergate passes there are increasingly strong reasons for asserting that some revisionism is justified. The important new research presented by the authors Len Colodny and Robert Gettlin in *Silent Coup* (1990) is one of those reasons. . . . All that can be said with certainty is, that the judgement of history on Watergate is a long way from being final.

Watergate began with the burglary at the Democratic National Committee Headquarters in the early hours of the morning on 17 June 1972. Although this was neither the original starting point nor the most pivotal episode in the drama, nevertheless the important unanswered question remains: 'Who ordered the break-in?'

The Watergate Break-in Was Not Nixon's Idea

The one fact that is now well established is that the order did not come from Nixon. After the most exhaustive investigations by the FBI, the Congress, and the office of the Special Prosecutor, not one single piece of evidence has emerged to suggest that the President gave any direct or indirect instructions for the break-in. There is nothing to confirm that he knew about it in advance or that he received any information from the bugging operation that preceded it. This exoneration does not depend, as Nixon's principal biographer Stephen Ambrose has uncharitably suggested, on the investigators' failure to uncover a memo that said, 'Break into the Watergate and bug Larry O'Brien—Richard Nixon'. Instead it relies on two propositions, both well supported by evidence. The first is that Nixon's immediate reactions to the break-in were consistent with ignorance of what had happened. The second is that there were other figures, in or extremely close to the White House, who had their own personal motives for ordering the break-in, and operated accordingly.

Nixon's first responses to the news of the burglary were those of surprise and cynicism, followed by a reflex action designed to ensure political damage limitation. The two men who were with him at Key Biscayne, Florida when he first heard about Watergate were his closest friends Bob Abplanalp and Bebe Rebozo. Both have given accounts of the President taking the call which came in from [Chief of Staff] Bob Haldeman on the morning of Sunday 18 June, reporting on the break-in. 'Hell, I was with him in the room', recalled Abplanalp. 'I heard him say, "They did WHAAT?" to Haldeman. He was so astonished he was practically shouting. He came off the phone shaking his head.' Rebozo has confirmed this atmosphere of mystification. 'First he was amazed. Then he sat down and laughed about it. He said two or three times, "What in God's name were we doing there?"' It seems improbable that Nixon would put on such an act for the benefit of his two best friends, or indeed for Haldeman, who was equally convinced at his end of the call that the President's surprise was genuine.

Nixon's next move was to telephone [Presidential Assistant] Charles Colson. 'I was suspect number one with the President', recalled Colson. 'At that time in my life I would have gladly organized the bugging of a political opponent, but the plain fact was I had nothing whatever to do with it. I think I got this through to the President, but my strongest memory of that call was his anger. He kept saying it was stupid. Over and over again he asked "Why? Why?"'

The initial presumption on which Nixon (and later everyone else) worked was that the break-in to the Democratic National Committee Headquarters must have been a bugging operation directed at the Democratic Party Chairman Lawrence F. O'Brien. Nixon was certainly interested in O'Brien's activities, particularly after Bebe Rebozo had passed on some evidence that O'Brien was receiving a large personal retainer from [wealthy eccentric] Howard Hughes. A financial connection with Hughes could be an albatross around the neck of any politician, as Nixon had learned to his cost in 1962 when the Democrats had raised hell over the Hughes loan to his brother Donald. So with the thought in the back of his mind of playing the Hughes card back against the Democrats, Nixon sent a memo to Haldeman asking for the story to be checked out.

January 14th 1971

ABOARD AIR FORCE ONE

To: H.R. Haldeman

From: The President

It would seem that the time is approaching when Larry O'Brien is held accountable for his retainer with Hughes. Bebe has some information on this although it is, of course, not solid but there is no question that one of Hughes's people did have O'Brien on a very heavy retainer for 'services rendered' in the past. Perhaps Colson should make a check on this.

Haldeman scribbled 'Let's try Dean' on the bottom of this memo and passed the assignment to the Counsel's office.

It is part of the mythology of Watergate that this presidential memo in January 1971 was the motivation for the break-in to the DNC offices eighteen months later. This is untrue. Dean and his team did try to investigate Rebozo's report, but got nowhere. However, six months later, an Internal Revenue Service contact of John Ehrlichman's came up with the information that O'Brien was receiving a consultancy fee of $160,000 a year from the Hughes Tool Corporation. Thus, by the middle of 1971, the request in Nixon's 14 January memo had been answered, although not through the Haldeman-Dean channel, whose efforts to find the information had fizzled out.

The Plot Was John Dean's

In fact, John Dean had an interest of his own in the DNC offices: in November 1971 he gave his two investigators, Jack Caulfield and Tony Ulasewicz, an intriguing order.

'Dean wants you to check the offices of the Democratic National Committee', Caulfield instructed Ulasewicz. The ex-policeman obeyed his instructions. Ulasewicz went over to the Watergate building and entered the DNC's headquarters. No break-in was necessary. Full access was achieved by the simple subterfuge of masquerading as a visitor. Ulasewicz walked all around the DNC's floor, noting the location of the various offices. 'It was a similar business office to what the Republicans would have, a place for records of donors, sending out brochures, making arrangements for dinners and fundraising programs, hiring people out in the field, contacts with newspapers and all the routine matters', he reported to Caulfield, adding: 'I don't know what you think is in this office. My street smarts told me when Dean's asking me this kind of thing, there's something that they are after. Something hot. I told him "It's not there".'

In the familiar accounts of Watergate, little or no attention has been paid to this strange episode of Ulasewicz 'casing the joint' at the DNC headquarters. His walk through, ordered by Dean, took place seven months before the 17 June 1972 break-in. At that time no other White House source or [Committee to Re-elect the President (CRP)] official had the faintest notion that the DNC headquarters was being targeted in this way. Nixon was oblivious of such an activity. Equally ignorant were John Mitchell, Jeb Magruder, Gordon Liddy and Howard Hunt. So if all the principal *dramatis personae* of the later break-in drama were unaware of this reconnaissance mission, what on earth was John Dean up to when he sent his investigators into the Watergate building in November 1971?

The answer to this question is stranger than fiction. Only a brief summary can be given here, although serious students of the preliminaries to Watergate are strongly recommended to immerse themselves in *Silent Coup* as required reading on this phase of the story. According to the authors of *Silent Coup*, Dean's interest in the DNC was based on prostitution rather than politics. He was desperately anxious to acquire hard information on leading Democrats sleeping with call girls. As we have seen, he had made an abortive effort to deal in this type of dirt earlier in 1971, when he acquired the 'Happy Hooker's' list of clients through an Ulasewicz operation. In the winter of 1971/2 he started to plan a similar dirt-digging project. The essence of his plan was to bug the telephones of certain junior employees of the Democratic National Committee whom Dean believed to be in the business of putting visiting politicians in touch with a Washington call-girl ring. The target, therefore, was not O'Brien's office, but offices on the other side of the building.

Operation Gemstone

Bugging these particular telephones required two break-ins. The two veterans of the Plumbers break-in, Howard Hunt and Gordon Liddy, became the masterminds of the operation. Liddy had by this time been appointed as Counsel to the Committee to Re-elect the President (CRP). In that role, at Dean's urging, Liddy had prepared a $1 million security and intelligence gathering plan called Operation Gemstone. He first unveiled it at a meeting in January 1972 attended by Dean, John Mitchell (who was about to become Chairman of CRP) and Jeb Magruder, who was to be Mitchell's deputy at CRP. Mitchell at first vetoed Gemstone, but Dean encouraged Liddy to resurrect it and to re-present it in a modified form at a further meeting on 30 March with Mitchell and Magruder.

Magruder's testimony as to what was said at this crucial meeting has been erratic. In the account he gave to the Senate Watergate Committee in 1973, Magruder claimed that Mitchell approved a scaled-down Gemstone operation and specifically authorised the burglary of the DNC offices in the Watergate building. But in his interview with the authors of *Silent Coup*, Magruder said Mitchell did not approve the DNC as a break-in target. 'The first plan we got had been initiated by Dean. Mitchell didn't do anything. All Mitchell did is just what I did, was acquiesce to

John Dean Speaks

White House Special Counsel John Dean tried to explain his role in Watergate in his memoirs.

For a thousand days I would serve as counsel to the President. I soon learned that to make my way upward, into a position of confidence and influence, I had to travel downward through factional power plays, corruption and finally outright crimes. Although I would be rewarded for diligence, true advancement would come from doing those things which built a common bond of trust—or guilt—between me and my superiors. In the Nixon White House, these upward and downward paths diverged, yet joined, like prongs of a tuning fork pitched to a note of expediency. Slowly, steadily, I would climb toward the moral abyss of the President's inner circle until I finally fell into it, thinking I had made it to the top just as I began to realize I had actually touched bottom.

John W. Dean III, *Blind Ambition: The White House Years.* New York: Simon and Schuster, 1996.

---

the pressure from the White House . . . The target never came from Mitchell.'

Magruder was undoubtedly in a tight spot at the time of the 30 March meeting. He was being relentlessly bullied by Liddy, whose charm offensive had recently taken the form of threats to tear his arm off. He was being pressed for a favourable decision on Gemstone by Dean, who claimed to have the White House behind him. As a character, Magruder was congenitally weak and anxious to please. Like a feather pillow, he gave way to the person who last sat on him. It was entirely in character for him to take the line of least resistance. As the authors of *Silent Coup* summarised his situation: 'Magruder was trapped between the pressure from Dean at the White House and Mitchell's repeated annoyed refusals to approve Gemstone on behalf of the CRP. So trapped, we believe, that Magruder gave the CRP's go-ahead to fund the scaled-down Gemstone without Mitchell's approval, using the funds that were already under Magruder's own control.'

The extension of Gemstone's electronic surveillance plans into the Watergate bugging operation again had Dean's fingerprints all over it. His principal motivation seems to have been his desire to gather intelligence on the link between the call-girl ring and the Democrats. A secondary motivation may have been his alleged wish to gain access to a call-girl address book and some compromising photographs in the desk of one particular DNC official.

The notion that the break-in that led to the President of the United States' downfall was all to do with John Dean seeking salacious gossip about call girls and Democrats seems, at first glance, impossibly far-fetched. Impressive though *Silent Coup*'s research has been in establishing the theory, this author would have hesitated in accepting it had it not been for Gordon Liddy.

Nixon Was Deceived

'Without doubt the man who commanded and conceived the Watergate operation was John Dean', said Liddy. 'Mitchell and Nixon had nothing whatever to do with it. I didn't realize that at the time. Like most other people I was fooled by Dean's facile lies. "Oh you don't understand Mitchell's ways", he told me when I was assuming from everything Mitchell said to me that he wanted Gemstone aborted. It was Dean who got the show on the road again. His meal ticket at the White House was to pass up the line the sort of who-sleeps-with-who-material that [FBI Director] J. Edgar Hoover used to feed the various Presidents.

That was Dean's level of sleaze. But he was a nasty, cunning little ferret so he didn't tell anyone except Howard Hunt that what he was really after was the call-girl address book and a bug on the phones that were used to book the call girls. He duped Magruder on that one and he duped me. I remember Magruder saying to me, "what we want is what they've got right here", pointing at the middle draw of his own desk. Now he didn't mean Larry O'Brien's desk. When the Cubans went in they didn't go near O'Brien's office in the DNC. Hunt gave them their orders and on the second break-in they went straight to the office and the desk of a secretary called Maxie Wells. Our look-out post from the hotel over the road was angled to that office not to O'Brien's . . . The whole damn Watergate break-in was Dean's show. All the evidence confirms it. I thought I was involved in an operation that was politically important to the President. I now know it was an operation that was personally important to John Dean. Period.'

If Gordon Liddy, in theory the physical commander of the Watergate break-in, was deceived in this way, how much greater must have been the deception of the President. As already recounted, Nixon was completely baffled when the first news of the break-in reached him in Key Biscayne on the morning of 18 June.

While his first reactions were those of ignorance, his secondary responses were those of anger towards some of his senior aides. That was sound, if misplaced, thinking. For the one member of his staff he never suspected of having anything to do with the burglary was John Dean. Yet it was to Dean, the true author of the Watergate break-in, that the President and his Chief of Staff turned for advice on the damage-limitation exercise that became the cover-up. That was a fatal error.

Nixon Resigned to Avoid Impeachment

Stanley I. Kutler

In the history of the United States, only two presidents have ever been impeached: Andrew Johnson in the 1860s and Bill Clinton in the 1990s. When Congress passes articles of impeachment, a president is, in effect, placed on trial. If two-thirds of the Senate finds the president guilty, he can be removed from office.

Richard Nixon faced the threat of impeachment in the summer of 1974. By that time the Watergate investigators had heard the Oval Office tape of June 23, 1972, which indicated that Nixon had been involved in the Watergate cover-up.

In the following selection from his book *The Wars of Watergate: The Last Crisis of Richard Nixon,* Stanley I. Kutler explores Nixon's decision to resign as president of the United States effective August 9, 1974. Even though he had stated in his January 1974 State of the Union Address that he would never resign, and even though he had many supporters, Nixon knew that he would lose any formal impeachment hearings in the Senate. In order to avoid further damage to the nation and to the Republican Party, writes Kutler, Nixon decided to step down. Kutler is the E. Gordon Fox Professor of American Institutions at the University of Wisconsin.

PRESIDENT NIXON APPEARED FOR HIS LAST CABINET MEETing on Tuesday, August 6. As usual, the staff prepared "talking points" for him. Whatever decisions had been reached—tentatively or firmly—the President dealt with

---

the group as he always had: as subordinates whom he needed to exhort to do their best in behalf of the Administration. He had, nevertheless, to confront the impeachment issue and give the Cabinet officers some indication of his course. He reminded his lieutenants that the presidency had experienced enormous trauma in the past decade, with the assassination of Kennedy and with Johnson "literally hounded from office." The institution, he said, must not sustain another "hammer blow" without a defense. Consequently, he would not resign, and would let the constitutional process run. This, he insisted, would be in the "best interests of the Nation"; he would not "desert the principles which give our government legitimacy." To do otherwise, he continued, "would be a regrettable departure from American historical principles." He offered nothing in the way of personal defense aside from past diplomatic triumphs; instead, he wrapped himself in the mantle of the presidency—claiming that he had no choice but to continue the route designed in the Constitution.

With that, Nixon turned to a discussion of economic problems, projecting policies for six months in the future. Attorney General William Saxbe was dumbfounded by Nixon's bravado. "Mr. President, don't you think we should be talking about next week, not next year?" he asked. According to Saxbe, Nixon looked around the table, no one said a word, and with that he picked up his papers and left the room.

Nixon Wanted Impeachment at First

The President's line was familiar. He had said in his January 1974 State of the Union message that he never would resign. He had told himself on numerous occasions that resignation could only be equated with guilt. In an interview with columnist James Kilpatrick in May, Nixon vehemently denied any intention of resigning. To do so, he said, would be to fatally weaken the presidency. Future presidents, he warned, would constantly be looking over their shoulders at Congress. Resignation or impeachment, he continued, would destabilize the nation and the world. Either path "would have the traumatic effect of destroying that sense of stability and leadership. And as far as this particular President is concerned, I will not be a party under any circumstances to any action which would set that kind of precedent."

Nixon thought then that he must let the impeachment process run its course because it would be "best for the country, our system of government, and the constitutional process." Two months later, Representative Caldwell Butler came to the same conclusion. Resignation offered only short-term benefits, Butler thought; more important, he did not want to establish a precedent "for harassment out of office, which is what would be claimed." He, too, wanted to follow the constitutional process: "It's a pretty good system." The President at that time gave every appearance of continuing in office. He asked an old friend to "leisurely" prepare a speech on world law and peace. Nixon wanted it as a radio address but then proposed a wide mail distribution. He planned the talk for August or September, and he emphasized there was no need for urgency.

Old friends weighed in with encouraging words. A New York lawyer exhorted Nixon not to resign and bitterly assailed "gutless Republicans" who had suggested such a course. She urged him to have the "courage and fortitude" to go through the constitutional process. Some religious supporters urged the same course but with a different twist which apparently received no consideration. The Reverend Norman Vincent Peale relayed and endorsed a message from the prominent Jewish Orthodox leader Rabbi Samuel Silver, of Cincinnati. The nation, Silver believed, wanted to "love" its President. "All he needs to say is that he is sorry for the whole thing, that he admits he didn't handle it too well, that he is only human and he regrets the bad habit of swearing, etc.; that he should have cracked down on any wrongdoing immediately, that he hates to hurt people; that all he asks is the forgiveness of the people." Silver added that the President need not act like a "worm." But he must offer "a good, honest, humble attitude of contrition."

Even after the revelations of the June 23, 1972, tape, the President received extraordinary gestures of support. A California restaurateur, who had sent the President $10,000 to help him pay his income taxes, offered to turn over his interest in twenty-nine restaurants to finance a defense. "I love Richard Nixon—he is the greatest President this country has ever had," he declared. An Indiana Republican Congressman offered the same sentiments on the *Today* television show on August 8. "Don't confuse me with the facts. I've got a closed mind," Representative Earl Landgrebe said in response to the question whether he would vote to impeach the President. He would "stick with" Nixon, even if "I have to be taken out of this building and shot. . . . President Nixon has been the greatest President this country has had." But after the "smoking gun" tape became public, James Kilpatrick could take no more. "I am close to tears," he wrote. "Nixon's duplicity is almost beyond bearing." Had he told the truth from the outset, Kilpatrick declared, Watergate would have been a nine-day wonder, Nixon would have been re-elected, and no more would have been heard of the affair. Kilpatrick had believed the President when he said he knew nothing of the cover-up and that he was not a crook. Now, he sadly concluded, "it no longer really matters. . . . My President is a liar. I wish he were a crook instead."

Nixon's Party and Staff Begin to Abandon Him

But Richard Nixon was nothing if not a seasoned political hand. He had heard rumors for months that congressional Republicans might view his resignation as a relief from the terrible onus of voting on impeachment and as the way to remove the President as a political albatross for the party. Nixon undoubtedly had put his personal concerns above those of his party; yet, for all his disdain, he knew that he still had to reckon with it as a force of political life. He knew that winning was everything, and he offered a political twist to the sports metaphors he often favored when he noted that generosity or magnanimity had little to do with the outcome of events: "[T]he burden of the wounded must be removed in order for the rest to survive." He knew that either he must remove that burden himself, or others would do it.

Resistance to the legal process, faith in the President, and contempt for their opponents characterized Nixon's inner circle almost to the end. Preventing the "death of a thousand cuts" seemed to be the rallying cry for the President's men. [Chief of Staff Alexander] Haig complained, however, that to some White House aides the slogan meant that Nixon should resign rather than suffer such a painful ordeal—the "pussy fire group," he contemptuously called them, comparing them to Vietnamese who would not stand and fight. Some in the White House felt besieged: "It was us against the world." Every day, it seemed, brought what [Special Assistant to the president] Stephen Bull called the "Oh, Shit Syndrome," meaning another revelation, another disclosure, another indictment. Some left, "either under handcuffs, [or] running for the hills," another aide recalled. But some, like Bull, believed the President would extricate himself—until Bull learned of the June 23 tape.

Still, Bull knew that the White House atmosphere was different; "things just were not happening," he recalled, and the blank pages of the presidential logs offer mute testimony to that fact. For some, like Richard Moore, there was now little to do aside from "long lunch hours." For Moore, it was a time of fear that his friends would go to prison or that he himself would be indicted. Others, like Alan Greenspan, saw the final days as a time to help the Presi-

The American Public Hears
About Nixon's Misdeeds

Jonathan Schell, a writer for the New Yorker *magazine, describes how the public reacted to the news of Watergate.*

At the moment when the President announced "major developments" in the Watergate case, the national process that was the investigation overwhelmed the national process that was the coverup. The events that followed were all the more astounding to the nation because, at just the moment when the coverup began to explode, the President, in the view of many observers, had been on the point of strangling the "obsolete" Constitutional system and replacing it with a Presidential dictatorship. One moment, he was triumphant and his power was apparently irresistible; the next moment, he was at bay. For in the instant the President made his announcement, the coverup cracked—not just the Watergate coverup but the broader coverup, which concealed the underground history of the last five years—and the nation suffered an inundation of news. The newspaper headlines now came faster and thicker than ever before in American history. The stories ran backward in time, and each day's newspaper told of some event a little further in the past as reporters traced the underground history to the early days of the Administration, and even into the terms of former Administrations. With the history of half a decade pouring out all at once, the papers were stuffed with more news than even the most diligent reader could absorb. Moreover, along with the facts, non-facts proliferated as the desperate men in the White House put out one false or distorted statement after another, so that each true fragment of the story was all but lost in a maze of deceptions, and each event, true or false, came up dozens of times, in dozens of versions, until the reader's mind was swamped. And, as if what was in the newspapers were not already too much, television soon started up, and, in coverage that was itself a full-time job to watch, presented first the proceedings of the Ervin committee and then the proceedings of the House Judiciary Committee, when it began to weigh the impeachment of the President. And, finally, in a burst of disclosure without anything close to a precedent in history, the tapes were revealed—and not just once but twice. The first set of transcripts was released by the White House and was doctored, and only the second set, which was released by the Judiciary Committee, gave an accurate account of the President's conversations.

As the flood of information flowed into the public realm, overturning the accepted history of recent years, the present scene was also transformed. The Vice-President was swept from office when his bribe-taking became known, but so rapid was the pace of events that his departure was hardly noticed. Each of the institutions of the democracy that had been menaced by the President—and all had been menaced—was galvanized into action in its turn: the press, the television networks, the Senate, the House of Representatives, and, finally, in a dispute over release of the tapes, the Supreme Court. The public, too, was at last awakened, when the President fired the Special Prosecutor whom he had appointed to look into the White House crimes. In an outpouring of public sentiment that, like so much else that happened at the time, had no precedent in the nation's history, millions of letters and telegrams poured in to Congress protesting the President's action. The time of letters sent by the President to himself was over, and the time of real letters from real people had come. No one of the democracy's institutions was powerful enough by itself to remove the President; the efforts of all were required—and only when those efforts were combined was he forced from office.

Jonathan Schell, *The Time of Illusion*. New York: Knopf, 1976.

dent, and, more important, as a time to serve the republic. Greenspan had consistently rejected offers of Administration positions, but near the end he became Chairman of the Council of Economic Advisers, fearing that "the normal process of government would deteriorate or even collapse" unless firm action were taken. Such advisers as Leonard Garment were "amazed" that the President continued to function as well as he did. Nixon, he remembered, "took it right to the end." Finally, for the President's family, of course, it was a mournful time, all the more difficult, apparently, because he could not bring himself to discuss the situation with them. "[W]e never sat down as a family to talk about Watergate," Julie Eisenhower [Nixon's daughter] wrote. For Nixon himself, it was a "nightmare" time.

The President Decides to Resign

Richard Nixon should be taken at his word. When he learned that Republicans and Southern Democrats had banded together to support impeachment, he knew he could not finish his second term. Thereafter, the only question concerned the manner of his leaving. He later wrote that he decided to resign just before the Judiciary Committee voted, meaning, of course, that his talk to his Cabinet on August 6 was pure sham. Other accounts suggest greater uncertainty in his decision. In these versions, Haig is a hero of sorts, a man who kept the President on the course of resignation, sparing the nation more agony. Haig himself may have been the source of such tales; John Mitchell thought that Haig need not write any account of Watergate: "Haig has already gilded the history. I don't think he has to write any more." Such accounts add a measure of drama, to be sure; yet they betray the history of a man who measured his career by a careful calculation of what was best for him. In all probability, Richard Nixon needed little push from others.

The President may have heard a favorable signal on

August 7, when Robert McClory told the White House congressional-liaison man that [House Judiciary Committee Chairman] Rodino had asked him to communicate his view that he had "absolutely no interest in pursuing any kind of criminal action against the President should he elect to resign." According to McClory, Rodino promised to end the impeachment inquiry as well if Nixon stepped down. Speaker Carl Albert concurred, although he added that he had no influence over the Special Prosecutor's course of action. The news from McClory undoubtedly had some appeal. If Nixon learned of that development, then he would have done so just prior to his meeting with [Republican Party leaders] Goldwater, Rhodes, and Scott. That conversation, taken together with the news from Rodino, might well have been influential. Rodino later proved to be as good as his word: he promptly closed down the inquiry after the resignation. Democrats were off the hook of carrying out the formal, irrevocable act of impeachment; moreover, any further action on their part would have reeked of vindictiveness and easily generated a counter-reaction of sympathy for the fallen President.

That evening Nixon began to work in earnest on his resignation speech and arranged to meet Vice President Ford the next day to discuss a transition. In that meeting, the President recommended that Ford retain Haig; the rest of the meeting was awkward, as both men seemed to understand, yet were unable to express, what was required of each.

The following night, Nixon saw more than forty long-time, steadfast supporters. "I just hope I haven't let you down," he told them. But he said later that he knew he had—as he had "let down the country . . . our system of government and the dreams of all those young people that ought to get into government. . . . I . . . let the American people down, and I have to carry that burden with me for the rest of my life." Earlier, he met with congressional leaders from both parties. He told them what he would say to the nation that evening: he had "lost his base" in Congress, and he believed the outcome of the impeachment process to be inevitable. Speaker Albert best remembered that Nixon never discussed the question of whether he had done wrong. Perhaps that was asking too much. Instead, the President broke down in tears.

Nixon's last full day in office proceeded routinely. He vetoed annual appropriations bills for the Agriculture Department and the Environmental Protection Agency on the grounds that they were inflationary. On a lesser, but far more symbolic note, he nominated a judge to fill a federal court seat in Wisconsin which had been vacant for three years. Nixon had sought unsuccessfully to appoint an old friend, Republican Representative Glenn Davis, but the American Bar Association, as well as state groups, had mounted an intense campaign in opposition. The new appointment on August 8 painfully measured the President's decline and powerlessness.

Later that day, Nixon addressed his simple letter of resignation to the keeper of the seals, the Secretary of State: "I hereby resign the Office of President of the United States."...

Nixon's Last Day as President

The President spent the afternoon of August 8 correcting and memorizing his resignation speech, to be broadcast that evening. "One thing, Ron, old boy," he feebly joked to [Press Secretary Ron] Ziegler, "we won't have to have any more press conferences, and we won't even have to tell them that[,] either!" Of course, he had said a similar thing a dozen years earlier in California. He also said that he looked forward to writing, noting that it might be done in prison. "Some of the best writing in history has been done in prison. Think of Lenin and Gandhi," he said.

At 9:00 P.M. the thirty-seventh President addressed the nation from the White House for the thirty-seventh time. Comparatively little of his talk had to do with Watergate and his resignation. If Richard Nixon were indeed to write from prison, first he would broadcast his own apologia. Watergate had been "a long and difficult period." He wished to carry on and persevere in the presidency, but events of the past few days convinced him that "I no longer have a strong enough political base in the Congress to justify continuing that effort." He wanted to "see the constitutional process through," but with the loss of his political base, he said, the process had been served, and there was no need to prolong it. Because of the Watergate situation, he contended, Congress would not give him the necessary support to govern effectively. With a hint of defiance, he asserted that he had never been a quitter. To resign was "abhorrent to every instinct" within him. But he would put "the interests of America first." America, he said, needed a full-time President and a full-time Congress; an impeachment battle would only drain both the institutions and the nation. "Therefore, I shall resign the Presidency effective at noon tomorrow," he added.

Nixon seemed sincere as he expressed hope that his act would heal the nation's wounds. And he offered what apparently he had not told the congressional leaders who had conferred with him: "I regret deeply any injuries that may have been done in the course of the events that led to this decision. I would say only that if some of my judgments were wrong—and some were wrong—they were made in what I believed at the time to be the best interest of the Nation." It was Richard Nixon's only moment that approximated contrition.

The rest of the talk focused on his achievements—the end of the Vietnam war, the opening to China, the conciliatory responses of the Arab nations to his diplomatic efforts, and the agreements with the Soviet Union. Nothing was said of any gains toward that domestic peace which Nixon had promised more than five years earlier. Finally, he insisted that resignation would not be his St. Helena;

rather, he promised that the nation would see more of him in the years to come.

The networks followed the President's resignation speech with the "instant analysis" that Nixon and Agnew had so bitterly assailed. Nixon undoubtedly savored the irony. Now, the commentators treated him generously—"a touch of class," "conciliatory," "few things in his presidency became him as much as his manner of leaving." He also would have heard more familiar chords. One commentator remarked: "From the viewpoint of Congress, that wasn't a very satisfactory speech." Nixon had expressed "regret," to be sure; but finally, the reason he gave for resigning was that Congress had deprived him of a "political base," making it impossible for him to continue in office. It was the opening salvo in his campaign for history.

Six years earlier, to the day, Nixon had delivered perhaps the best speech of his career as he accepted the Republican presidential nomination. He had told the nation that he would restore respect for the law. "Time is running out," he said at that time, "for the merchants of crime and corruption in American society."

Nixon's Departure from the White House

The morning after his resignation announcement, the President gave another speech, a "spontaneous thing," he called it, as he spoke in the East Room of the White House to an assembled group of White House and Administration workers. As often before in his career, Nixon was anxious to bare his soul—never more so than in this, his darkest hour, and perhaps the darkest hour of the American presidency. But it was the wrong time. Now, the time was more appropriate for a quiet fade-out—unless he had another goal in mind. Perhaps he did. The Friday morning talk marked the flip side of the speech the night before— different words, yet all part of the same album designed to impress indelibly the image of Richard Nixon as a man grievously wronged and a man not about to leave the public stage forever. It was, he said, "a beginning."

In the open society of America, the most private of moments often become the most public of spectacles. When a president embraces his family, visits the Lincoln Memorial, or receives a foreign visitor, we know the probing eye of the television camera will accompany him not only to give us "news," but to allow us vicariously to experience the event itself. Richard Nixon's last appearance before White House workers and Administration loyalists seemed, by its nature, a private event. The President could have conducted it in private, had he preferred. His family, he admitted, protested that "after all the agony television had caused us, its prying eye should [not] be allowed to intrude on this last and most intimate moment of all." But he sensed an opportunity to serve himself and seized the moment. "That's the way it has to be," he told them, adding that he owed it to his supporters and to the people. His daughter dutifully found her name mark on the floor. Clearly, Nixon would persist in his unceasing quest for gaining love and understanding from America. Spontaneous? In all likelihood, the occasion had all the spontaneity of a pointillist painting.

Nixon had home adversity through the years, sometimes with grace, other times with petulance, but always with verve. As he prepared to depart from office, he was reconciled to the inevitability of his punishment. The moment presented him with the opportunity to display a rarely seen introspective side of himself. Whether wallowing in the banality of self-pity or reciting his achievements with a feisty grit and pride, he remained a compelling phenomenon to admirers and adversaries alike.

APPENDIX

Excerpts from Original Documents

Document 1: Nixon's Environmental Plan

In his 1970 State of the Union message, Nixon made it clear that he believed that the time had come for the national government to take action on the environment. He also claimed that environmental regulation could be reconciled with the interests of business.

The great question of the seventies is, shall we surrender to our surroundings, or shall we make our peace with nature and begin to make reparations for the damage we have done to our air, to our land and to our water?

Restoring nature to its natural state is a cause beyond party and beyond factions. It has become a common cause of all the people of this country. It is a cause of particular concern to young Americans—because they more than we will reap the grim consequences of our failure to act on programs which are needed now if we are to prevent disaster later.

Clean air, clean water, open spaces—these should once again be the birthright of every American. If we act now—they can be.

We still think of air as free. But clean air is not free, and neither is clean water. The price tag on pollution control is high. Through our years of past carelessness we incurred a debt to nature, and now that debt is being called.

The program I shall propose to Congress will be the most comprehensive and costly program in this field in America's history.

It is not a program for just one year. A year's plan in this field is no plan at all. This is a time to look ahead not a year, but five years or ten years—whatever time is required to do the job.

I shall propose to this Congress a ten billion dollar nationwide clean waters program to put modern municipal waste treatment plants in every place in America where they are needed to make our waters clean again, and do it now.

We have the industrial capacity, if we begin now, to build them all within five years. This program will get them built within five years.

As our cities and suburbs relentlessly expand, those priceless open spaces needed for recreation areas accessible to their people are swallowed up—often forever. Unless we preserve these spaces while they are still available, we will have none to preserve. Therefore, I shall propose new financing methods for purchasing open space and park lands, now, before they are lost to us.

The automobile is our worst polluter of the air. Adequate control requires further advances in engine design and fuel composition. We shall intensify our research, set increasingly strict standards and strengthen enforcement procedures—and we shall do it now.

We no longer can afford to consider air and water common property, free to be abused by anyone without regard to the consequences. Instead, we should begin now to treat them as scarce resources, which we are no more free to contaminate than we are free to throw garbage into our neighbor's yard. This requires comprehensive new regulations. It also requires that, to the extent possible, the price of goods should be made to include the costs of producing and disposing of them without damage to the environment.

Now I realize that the argument is often made that a fundamental contradiction has arisen between economic growth and the quality of life, so that to have one we must forsake the other.

The answer is not to abandon growth, but to redirect it. For example, we should turn toward ending congestion and eliminating smog [with] the same reservoir of inventive genius that created them in the first place.

Continued vigorous economic growth provides us with the means to enrich life itself and to enhance our planet as a place hospitable to man.

Each individual must enlist in this fight if it is to be won.

Richard Nixon, 1970 State of the Union address, January 22, 1970.

Document 2: The Environmental Protection Agency

As president, Nixon preferred centralized institutions under his authority to congressional bodies or the federal bureaucracy. In a July 9, 1970, message to Congress, Nixon announced the establishment of one such institution, the Environmental Protection Agency, to coordinate environmental action.

TO THE CONGRESS OF THE UNITED STATES:

As concern with the condition of our physical environment has intensified, it has become increasingly clear that we need to know more about the total environment—land, water and air. It also has become increasingly clear that only by reorganizing our Federal efforts can we develop that knowledge, and effectively ensure the protection, development and enhancement of the total environment itself.

The Government's environmentally-related activities have grown up piecemeal over the years. The time has come to organize them rationally and systematically. As a major step in this direction, I am transmitting today two reorganization plans: one to establish an Environmental Protection Agency, and one to establish, within the Department of Commerce, a National Oceanic and Atmospheric Administration.

Our national government today is not structured to make a coordinated attack on the pollutants which debase the air we breathe, the water we drink, and the land that grows our food. Indeed, the present governmental structure for dealing with environmental pollution often defies effective and concerted action.

Despite its complexity, for pollution control purposes the environment must be perceived as a single, interrelated system. Present assignments of departmental responsibilities do not reflect this interrelatedness.

Many agency missions, for example, are designed primarily along media lines—air, water, and land. Yet the sources of air, water, and land pollution are interrelated and often interchangeable. A single source may pollute the air with smoke and chemicals, the land with solid wastes, and a river or lake with chemical and other wastes. Control of the air pollution may produce more solid wastes, which then pollute the land or water. Control of the water-polluting effluent may convert it into solid wastes, which must be disposed of on land.

Similarly, some pollutants—chemicals, radiation, pesticides—appear in all media. Successful control of them at present requires the coordinated efforts of a variety of separate agencies and departments. The results are not always successful.

A far more effective approach to pollution control would:

• Identify pollutants.

• Trace them through the entire ecological chain, observing and recording changes in form as they occur.

• Determine the total exposure of man and his environment.

• Examine interactions among forms of pollution.

• Identify where in the ecological chain interdiction would be most appropriate.

In organizational terms, this requires pulling together into one agency a variety of research, monitoring, standard-setting and enforcement activities now scattered through several departments and agencies. It also requires that the new agency include sufficient support elements—in research and in aids to State and local anti-pollution programs, for example—to give it the needed strength and potential for carrying out its mission. The new agency would also, of course, draw upon the results of research conducted by other agencies.

Richard Nixon, address to Congress, July 9, 1970.

Document 3: Student Protesters Should Change Their Tactics

Nixon greatly disapproved of the violence of many protests conducted by university students against the war in Vietnam. In a speech made in April, 1970, he said that while he valued students' opinions, he thought they should express them peacefully.

... I have decided to speak briefly on a subject of very great concern to all of you, of very great concern to me, and I will say to all Americans at this time. I refer to the problems of education in the very broadest sense in the United States. ...

That is the problem of what I would call the new revolutionary spirit and new revolutionary actions that are taking place on the campuses of many of our colleges and universities and also that may begin to take place, and also are taking place, I understand, in some of the high schools of this country.

Now I am not going to speak to that problem in the way that you might usually expect. It is easy to be against some of the actions that have occurred. All of us are concerned by those actions. We are against them. The question is to refine our discussions to some simple issues and some simple principles. I am going to state some opinions now that are my own. ...

First, with regard to that great problem of dissent on the college and university campuses, let us recognize that this is a very healthy force when we consider it at its best. We do not want, in America, an educational system which becomes ingrown, stultified, loses the ability to develop the new ideas to keep pace with the change in our very fast-changing society.

Consequently, we can be thankful today that we do have a younger generation, which is as I have often said, with all of the faults that we may see in it, the best-educated younger generation that we have ever had; more deeply motivated than any that we have ever had; one that deeply cares about America, about our system, and about our educational system. We may not agree with them, but they do care. ...

Then we come to the second point: That is the method of dissent. Here again, we have some fine lines that need to be drawn and some principles that we must have in mind.

There are those who believe that any means are justified, if the end is worthwhile. And all of us, again, if we remember the past, will, of course, agree that we can never adopt that principle, because when we adopt that principle of any means to the end, the end eventually becomes the means.

So we look at our college campuses and our university campuses today and we see some things which concern us. We see, first, the dissent. That we accept, we welcome, and we encourage, provided it is the peaceful kind of dissent within the rules of an institution and of our society.

And, second, we also—and I presently today proclaim as I have previously the principle that we do not want to have the Federal Government of this country running our institutions. We do not want them interfering with our colleges and our universities. It is their responsibility to provide education in an independent, free way in the American tradition.

But, third, we have another factor that we must face. That is this: When we find situations in numbers of colleges and universities which reach the point where students in the name of dissent and in the name of change terrorize other students and faculty members, when they rifle files, when they engage in violence, when they carry guns and knives in the classrooms, then I say it is time for faculties, boards of trustees and school administrators to have the backbone to stand up against this kind of situation.

Excerpted from Richard Nixon, address to the Chamber of Commerce of the United States, April 29, 1970.

Document 4: Explaining the Invasion of Cambodia

In the face of a huge public outcry, Nixon tried to justify American participation in the South Vietnamese invasion of Cambodia in a televised speech on June 3, 1970. He claimed that the invasion was necessary in order to prevent a longer, more destructive war. He also pointed out that, despite the invasion, he was continuing to withdraw American troops from Vietnam.

Good evening, my fellow Americans.

One month ago, I announced a decision ordering American participation with South Vietnamese forces in a series of operations against Communist-occupied areas in Cambodia which have been used for five years as bases for attacks on our forces in South Vietnam.

This past weekend, in the Western White House in California, I met with Secretary Laird, General Abrams and other senior advisors to receive a firsthand report on the progress of this operation.

Based on General Abrams' report, I can now state that this has been the most successful operation of this long and very difficult war.

Before going into the details which form the basis for this conclusion, I believe it would be helpful to review briefly why I considered it necessary to make this decision, what our objectives were, and the prospects for achieving those objectives.

You will recall that on April 20, I announced the withdrawal of an additional 150,000 American troops from Vietnam within a year—which will bring the total number withdrawn, since I have taken office, to 260,000. I also reaffirmed on that occasion our proposals for a negotiated peace.

At the time of this announcement I warned that if the enemy tried to take advantage of our withdrawal program by increased attacks in Cambodia, Laos, or South Vietnam in a way that endangered the lives of our men remaining in South Vietnam, that I would, in my capacity as Commander-in-Chief of our Armed Forces, take strong action to deal with that threat.

Between April 20 and April 30, Communist forces launched a series of attacks against a number of key cities in neutral Cambodia. Their objective was unmistakable—to link together bases they had maintained in Cambodia for five years in violation of Cambodian neutrality. The entire six-hundred-mile Cambodian–South Vietnam border would then have become one continuous hostile territory from which to launch assaults upon American and allied forces.

This posed an unacceptable threat to our remaining forces in South Vietnam. It would have meant higher casualties. It would have jeopardized our program for troop withdrawals. It would have meant a longer war. And—carried out in the face of an explicit warning from this Government—failure to deal with the enemy action would have eroded the credibility of the United States before the entire world.

After very intensive consultations with my top advisors, I directed that American troops join the South Vietnamese in destroying these major enemy bases along the Cambodian frontier. I said when I made this announcement: "Our purpose is not to occupy these areas. Once the enemy forces are driven out of the sanctuaries and once their supplies are destroyed, we will withdraw."

That pledge is being kept. I said further on that occasion, "We take this action not for the purpose of expanding the war in Cambodia, but for the purpose of ending the war in Vietnam."

Richard Nixon, televised speech on the U.S. operation in Cambodia, June 3, 1970.

Document 5: Nixon Calls on His Silent Majority

In a November 3, 1970 speech, Nixon asked the American people to unite themselves behind his Vietnamization policy. While a "vocal minority" stood in opposition to the war, Nixon pointed out, he believed that the "silent majority" of Americans stood behind him and his policies.

My fellow Americans, I am sure you recognize from what I have said that we really only have two choices open to us if we want to end this war.

I can order an immediate, precipitate withdrawal of all Americans from Vietnam without regard to the effects of that action.

Or we can persist in our search for a just peace through a negotiated settlement if possible, or through continued implementation of our plan for Vietnamization if necessary—a plan in which we will withdraw all of our forces from Vietnam on a schedule in accordance with our program, as the South Vietnamese become strong enough to defend their own freedom.

I have chosen the second course.

It is not the easy way.

It is the right way.

It is a plan which will end the war and serve the cause of peace—not just in Vietnam but in the Pacific and in the world.

In speaking of the consequences of a precipitate withdrawal, I mentioned that our allies would lose confidence in America.

Far more dangerous, we would lose confidence in ourselves. The immediate reaction would be a sense of relief that our men were coming home. But as we saw the consequences of what we had done, inevitable remorse and divisive recrimination would scar our spirit as a people. . . .

I recognize that some of my fellow citizens disagree with the plan for peace I have chosen. Honest and patriotic Americans have reached different conclusions as to how peace should be achieved.

In San Francisco a few weeks ago, I saw demonstrators carrying signs reading: "Lose in Vietnam, bring the boys home."

Well, one of the strengths of our free society is that any American has a right to reach that conclusion and to advocate that point of view. But as President of the United States, I would be untrue to my oath of office if I allowed the policy of this nation to be dictated by the minority who hold that point of view and who try to impose it on the nation by mounting demonstrations in the street.

For almost 200 years, the policy of this nation has been made under our Constitution by those leaders in the Congress and in the White

House selected by all of the people. If a vocal minority, however fervent its cause, prevails over reason and the will of the majority this nation has no future as a free society.

And now I would like to address a word if I may to the young people of this nation who are particularly concerned, and I understand why they are concerned about this war.

I respect your idealism.

I share your concern for peace.

I want peace as much as you do.

There are powerful personal reasons I want to end this war. This week I will have to sign 83 letters to mothers, fathers, wives and loved ones of men who have given their lives for America in Vietnam. It is very little satisfaction to me that this is only one third as many letters as I signed the first week in office. There is nothing I want more than to see the day come when I do not have to write any of those letters.

I want to end the war to save the lives of those brave young men in Vietnam.

But I want to end it in a way which will increase the chance that their younger brothers and their sons will not have to fight in some future Vietnam someplace in the world.

And I want to end the war for another reason. I want to end it so that the energy and dedication of you, our young people, now too often directed into bitter hatred against those responsible for the war, can be turned to the great challenges of peace, a better life for all Americans, a better life for all people on this earth. . . .

And so tonight—to you, the great silent majority of my fellow Americans—I ask for your support.

Richard Nixon, televised address on plan for Vietnamization, November 3, 1970.

Document 6: Frustration with Watergate

In a press conference held on August 22, 1972, Nixon expressed his frustration over the constant attention the press paid to Watergate. He was particularly unhappy with questions over whether he would resign. Watergate, he asserted, was an unfortunate matter but he could no longer allow it to get in the way of his doing the business of the American people.

Q: Mr. President, at any time during the Watergate crisis did you ever consider resigning, and would you consider resigning if you felt that your capacity to govern had been seriously weakened? And in that connection, how much do you think your capacity to govern has been weakened?

The President: The answer to the first two questions is no; the answer to the third question is that it is true that as far as the capacity to govern is concerned, that to be under a constant barrage—12 to 15 minutes a night on each of the three major networks for 4 months— tends to raise some questions in the people's mind with regard to the President, and it may raise some questions with regard to the capacity to govern. But I also know this: I was elected to do a job. Watergate is an episode that I deeply deplore, and had I been running the campaign rather than trying to run the country, and particularly the foreign policy of this country at this time, it would never have happened. But that is water under the bridge, it is gone now.

The point that I make now is that we are proceeding as best we know how to get all those guilty brought to justice in Watergate. But now we must move on from Watergate to the business of the people, and the business of the people is continuing with initiatives we began in the first Administration.

Q: Mr. President.

The President: Just a moment.

We have had 30 minutes of this press conference. I have yet to have, for example, one question on the business of the people, which shows you how we are consumed with this. I am not criticizing the members of the press, because you naturally are very interested in this issue, but let me tell you, years from now people are going to perhaps be interested in what happened in terms of the efforts of the United States to build a structure of peace in the world. They are perhaps going to be interested in the efforts of this Administration to have a kind of prosperity that we have not had since 1955—that is, prosperity without war and without inflation—because throughout the Kennedy years and throughout the Johnson years, whatever prosperity we had was at the cost of either inflation or war or both. I don't say that critically of them, I am simply saying we have got to do better than that.

Now, our goal is to move forward then, to move forward to build a structure of peace. And when you say, do I consider resigning, the answer is no, I shall not resign. I have 3½ years to go, or almost 3½ years, and I am going to use every day of those 3½ years trying to get the people of the United States to recognize that, whatever mistakes we have made, that in the long run this Administration, by making this world safer for their children, and this Administration, by making their lives better at home for themselves and their children, deserves high marks rather than low marks. Now, whether I succeed or not, we can judge then.

Quoted in *The Nixon Presidential Press Conferences*, New York: Earl M. Coleman Enterprises, 1978.

Document 7: A Promise to Work for Peace

At the conclusion of his Chinese visit in February 1972, Nixon, along with his Chinese counterparts, released a joint statement of their intentions from the city of Shanghai. Both promised not only to normalize diplomatic relations between China and the United States but also to use their strengths to preserve peace rather than foment conflict.

There are essential differences between China and the United States in their social systems and foreign policies. However, the two sides agreed that countries, regardless of their social systems, should conduct their relations on the principles of respect for the sovereignty and territorial integrity of all states, nonaggression against other states, noninterference in the internal affairs of other states, equality and mutual benefit, and peaceful coexistence. International disputes should be settled on this basis, without resorting to the use or threat of force. The United States and the People's Republic of China are prepared to apply these principles to their mutual relations.

With these principles of international relations in mind the two sides stated that:

- Progress toward the normalization of relations between China and the United States is in the interests of all countries;
- Both wish to reduce the danger of international military conflict,
- Neither should seek hegemony in the Asia-Pacific region and each is opposed to efforts by any other country or group of countries to establish such hegemony; and
- Neither is prepared to negotiate on behalf of any third party or to enter into agreements or understandings with the other directed at other states.

Both sides are of the view that it would be against the interests of the peoples of the world for any major country to collude with another against other countries, or for major countries to divide up the world into spheres of interest.

The President's Trip to China, ed. Richard Wilson, New York: Bantam Books, 1972.

Document 8: Nixon Renounces "a Generation of Hostility"

On February 28, 1972, in a speech made upon his return from China, Nixon claimed that the major goals for his visit were first, to prevent another Asian conflict in which Americans would be involved, and second, to re-establish normal diplomatic relations with the People's Republic after twenty years of isolation. He was proud to say he had begun to achieve those goals.

When I announced this trip last July, I described it as a journey for peace. In the last thirty years Americans have in three different wars gone off in the hundreds of thousands to fight and some to die, in Asia and in the Pacific.

One of the central motives behind my journey to China was to prevent that from happening a fourth time to another generation of Americans.

As I've often said, peace means more than the mere absence of war. In a technical sense we were at peace with the People's Republic of China before this trip. But a gulf of almost 12,000 miles and twenty-two years of noncommunication and hostility separated the United States of America from the 750 million people who live in the People's Republic of China—and that's one-fourth of all the people in the world.

As a result of this trip we have started the long process of building a bridge across that gulf, and even now we have something better than the mere absence of war.

Not only have we completed a week of intensive talks at the highest levels, we have set up a procedure whereby we can continue to have discussions in the future.

We have demonstrated that nations with very deep and fundamental differences can learn to discuss those differences calmly, rationally, and frankly without compromising their principles.

This is the basis of a structure for peace; where we can talk about differences rather than fight about them.

The primary goal of this trip was to reestablish communication with the People's Republic of China after a generation of hostility. We achieved that goal.

The President's Trip to China, ed. Richard Wilson, New York: Bantam Books, 1972.

Document 9: A Peace With Honor in Vietnam

On January 23, 1973, Nixon announced the end of American participation in the Vietnam War with the signing of the Paris Peace Accords. All American troops would be withdrawn, and American prisoners of war would be released. In addition, the agreement promised to protect the Vietnamese regime of President Nguyen Van Thieu. Nixon thanked Americans for helping him to achieve what he believed was an honorable peace.

In the settlement that has now been agreed to, all the conditions that I laid down then have been met. A cease-fire, internationally supervised, will begin at 7 p.m. this Saturday, January 27th, Washington time.

Within 60 days from this Saturday, all Americans held prisoners of war throughout Indochina will be released. There will be the fullest possible accounting for all of those who are missing in action.

During the same 60-day period, all American forces will be withdrawn from South Vietnam.

The people of South Vietnam have been guaranteed the right to determine their own future, without outside interference.

By joint agreement, the full text of the agreement and the protocols to carry it out, will be issued tomorrow.

Throughout these negotiations we have been in the closest consultation with President Thieu and other representatives of the Republic of Vietnam. This settlement meets the goals and has the full support of President Thieu and the Government of the Republic of Vietnam, as well as that of our other allies who are affected.

The United States will continue to recognize the Government of the Republic of Vietnam as the sole legitimate government of South Vietnam.

We shall continue to aid South Vietnam within the terms of the agreement and we shall support efforts by the people of South Vietnam to settle their problems peacefully among themselves.

We must recognize that ending the war is only the first step toward building the peace. All parties must now see to it that this is a peace that lasts, and also a peace that heals, and a peace that not only ends the war in Southeast Asia, but contributes to the prospects of peace in the whole world.

This will mean that the terms of the agreement must be scrupulously adhered to. We shall do everything the agreement requires of us and we shall expect the other parties to do everything it requires of them. We shall also expect other interested nations to help insure that the agreement is carried out and peace is maintained. . . .

And finally, to all of you who are listening, the American People: Your steadfastness in supporting our insistence on peace with honor has made peace with honor possible. I know that you would not have wanted that peace jeopardized. With our secret negotiations at the sensitive stage they were in during this recent period, for me to have discussed publicly our efforts to secure peace would not only have violated our understanding with North Vietnam; it would have seriously harmed and possibly destroyed the chances for peace. Therefore, I know that you now can understand why, during these past several weeks, I have not made any public statements about those efforts.

The important thing was not to talk about peace; but to get peace and to get the right kind of peace. This we have done.

Now that we have achieved an honorable agreement, let us be proud that America did not settle for a peace that would have betrayed our allies, that would have abandoned our prisoners of war, that would have ended the war for us but would have continued the war for the 50 million people of Indochina. Let us be proud of the 2-½ million young Americans who served in Vietnam, who served with honor and distinction in one of the most selfless enterprises in the history of nations. And let us be proud of those who have sacrificed, who gave their lives so that the people of South Vietnam might live in freedom and so that the world might live in peace.

Richard Nixon, televised announcement on the Vietnam peace agreement, January 23, 1970.

Document 10: Nixon Asserts Control Over the White House Tapes

The tapes of Nixon's White House conversations were sought by all of the institutions that were investigating Watergate by the Spring of 1974, including the House Judiciary Committee. Nixon was very slow to release the tapes. He claimed that he was protected by executive privilege; a president had to be able to keep secrets for the sake of national security.

Good evening. I have asked for this time tonight in order to announce my answer to the House Judiciary Committee's subpoena for additional Watergate tapes and to tell you something about the action I shall be taking tomorrow, about what I hope they will mean to you, and about the very difficult choices that were presented to me.

These actions will at last once and for all show that what I knew and what I did with regard to the Watergate break-in and cover-up were just as I have described them to you from the very beginning. I spent many hours during the past few weeks thinking about what I would say to the American people if I were to reach the decision I shall announce tonight. And so my words have not been lightly chosen. I can assure you they are deeply felt.

It was almost two years ago in June, 1972, that five men broke into the Democratic National Committee headquarters in Washington.

It turned out that they were connected with my reelection committee, and the Watergate break-in became a major issue in the campaign.

The full resources of the F.B.I. and the Justice Department were used to investigate the incident thoroughly.

I instructed my staff and campaign aides to cooperate fully with the investigation. The F.B.I. conducted nearly 1,500 interviews.

For nine months, until March, 1973, 1 was assured by those charged with conducting and monitoring the investigations that no one in the White House was involved.

Nevertheless, for more than a year there have been allegations, insinuations, that I knew about the planning of the Watergate break-in and that I was involved in an extensive plot to cover it up. . . .

Many people assumed that the tapes must incriminate the President, or that otherwise he wouldn't insist on their privacy. But the problem I confronted was this: Unless a President can protect the privacy of the advice he gets, he cannot get the advice he needs.

This principle is recognized in the constitutional doctrine of executive privilege, which has been defended and maintained by every President since Washington and which has been recognized by the courts whenever tested as inherent in the Presidency.

I consider it to be my constitutional responsibility to defend this principle.

Richard Nixon, address to the nation, April 29, 1974.

Document 11: The Taped Conversation in Which Nixon Approves the Watergate Cover-Up

After two years of denials, Nixon finally admitted his involvement in the Watergate cover-up when the tapes of his Oval Office conversations of July 23, 1972 were released in the summer of 1974. In conversations with chief of staff H.R. Haldeman, Nixon can be heard approving a plan to put pressure on Pat Gray, acting FBI director, and Vernon Walters, deputy CIA director, to stop the investigations of the Watergate break-in. The tape of this "smoking gun" conversation confirmed that Nixon had obstructed justice.

HALDEMAN: OK, that's fine. Now, on the investigation, you know, the Democratic break-in thing, we're back to the . . . problem area because the FBI is not under control, because Gray doesn't exactly know how to control them, and . . . their investigation is now leading into some productive areas, because they've been able to trace the money, not through the money itself, but through the bank. . . . [A]nd it goes in some directions we don't want it to go. . . . [T]here have been some things, like an informant came in off the street to the FBI in Miami, who was a photographer, or has a friend who is a photographer who developed some films through this guy [Watergate burglar Bernard] Barker, and the films had pictures of Democratic National Committee letterhead[s]. . . . Mitchell came up with yesterday, and John Dean analyzed very carefully last night and concludes—concurs—now with

Mitchell's recommendation that the only way to solve this . . . is for us to have [Deputy CIA Director Vernon] Walters call Pat Gray and just say, "Stay the hell out of this . . . this is ah, business here we don't want you to go any further on it." That's not an unusual development. . . .

PRESIDENT NIXON: What about Pat Gray, you mean he doesn't want to?

HALDEMAN: Pat does want to. He doesn't know how to, and he doesn't have, he doesn't have any basis for doing it. Given this, he will then have the basis. He'll call Mark Felt in, and the two of them . . . and Mark Felt wants to cooperate because—

PRESIDENT NIXON: Yeah.

HALDEMAN: —he's ambitious.

PRESIDENT NIXON: Yeah.

HALDEMAN: He'll call him in and say, "We've got the signal from across the river to, to put the hold on this." And that will fit rather well because the FBI agents who are working the case, at this point, feel that's what it is. This is CIA.

PRESIDENT NIXON: But they've traced the money to 'em.

HALDEMAN: Well they have, they've traced to a name, but they haven't gotten to the guy yet.

PRESIDENT NIXON: Would it be somebody here?

HALDEMAN: Ken Dahlberg [who worked for prominent contributor Dwayne Andreas].

PRESIDENT NIXON: Who the hell is Ken Dahlberg?

HALDEMAN: He's, he gave $25,000 in Minnesota and the check went directly in to this, to this guy, Barker.

PRESIDENT NIXON: Maybe he's a . . . bum. He didn't get this from the committee though, from Stans?

HALDEMAN: Yeah. It is. It is. It's directly traceable and there's some more through some Texas people in—that went to the Mexican bank which they can also trace to the Mexican bank. . . . They'll get their names today. . . .

PRESIDENT NIXON: I'm just thinking if they don't cooperate, what do they say? They, they, they were approached by the Cubans? That's what Dahlberg has to say, the Texans too. Is that the idea?

HALDEMAN: Well, if they will. But then we're relying on more and more people all the time. That's the problem. And they'll stop if we could, if we take this other step.

PRESIDENT NIXON: All right. Fine.

HALDEMAN: And, and they seem to feel the thing to do is get them to stop.

PRESIDENT NIXON: Right, fine.

HALDEMAN: They say the only way to do that is from White House instructions. And it's got to be to Helms and what's his name? [Deputy CIA Director General Vernon] Walters?

PRESIDENT NIXON: Walters.

HALDEMAN: And the proposal would be that Ehrlichman and I call him.

PRESIDENT NIXON: All right, fine. . . .

HALDEMAN: The FBI interviewed Colson yesterday. They determined that would be a good thing to do. . . . An interrogation, which he did, and that, the FBI guys working the case had concluded that there are one or two possibilities: one, that this was a White House [operation], they don't think that there is anything at the Election Committee—they think it was either a White House operation and they had some obscure reasons for it. . . . Or it was a—

PRESIDENT NIXON: Cuban thing—

HALDEMAN: —Cubans and the CIA. And after their interrogation of—

PRESIDENT NIXON: Colson.

HALDEMAN: —Colson, yesterday, they concluded it was not the White House, but are now convinced it's the CIA thing, so the CIA turnoff would—

PRESIDENT NIXON: Well, not sure of their analysis, I'm not going to get that involved. . . .

HALDEMAN: No, sir. We don't want you to.

PRESIDENT NIXON: You call them in. Good. Good deal. Play it tough. That's the way they play it and that's the way we are going to play it.

HALDEMAN: O.K. We'll do it.

Quoted in *Abuse of Power: The New Nixon Tapes*, ed. Stanley I. Kutler, New York: Free Press, 1997.

Document 12: The Articles of Impeachment Against Nixon

On July 30, 1974, the Judiciary Committee of the House of Representatives approved three articles of impeachment against Richard Nixon. Finally, after months of accusations and investigations, the government was ready to put Nixon on trial for his alleged actions over Watergate. If found guilty of those crimes, he would be removed from office.

Article I

In his conduct of the office of President of the United States, Richard M. Nixon, in violation of his constitutional oath faithfully to execute the office of President of the United States and, to the best of his ability, preserve, protect and defend the Constitution of the United States, and in violation of his constitutional duty to take care that the laws be faithfully executed, has prevented, obstructed, and impeded the administration of justice, in that:

On June 17, 1972, and prior thereto, agents of the Committee for the Re-election of the President:

Committed unlawful entry of the headquarters of the Democratic National Committee in Washington, District of Columbia, for the purpose of securing political intelligence. Subsequent thereto, Richard M. Nixon using the powers of his high office, engaged personally and through his subordinates and agents, in a course of conduct or plan designed to delay, impede, and obstruct the investigation of such unlawful entry; to cover up, conceal and protect those responsible; and to conceal the existence and scope of other unlawful covert activities. . . .

Article II
Using the powers of the office of President of the United States, Richard M. Nixon, in violation of his constitutional oath faithfully to execute the office of President of the United States, and to the best of his ability preserve, protect and defend the Constitution of the United States and, in disregard of his constitutional duty to take care that the laws be faithfully executed, has repeatedly engaged in conduct violating the constitutional right of citizens, impairing the due and proper administration of justice in the conduct of lawful inquiries, or contravening the laws of governing agencies of the executive branch and the purposes of these agencies. . . .

Article III
In his conduct of the office of President of the United States, Richard M. Nixon, contrary to his oath faithfully to execute the office of President of the United States and, to the best of his ability, to preserve, protect and defend the Constitution of the United States, and in violation of his constitutional duty to take care that the laws be faithfully executed, has failed without lawful cause or excuse to produce papers and things as directed by duly authorized subpoenas issued by the Committee on the Judiciary of the House of Representatives on April 11, 1974, May 15, 1974, May 30, 1974, and June 24, 1974, and willfully disobeyed such subpoenas.

The subpoenaed papers and things were deemed necessary by the committee in order to resolve by direct evidence fundamental, factual questions relating to Presidential direction, knowledge or approval of actions demonstrated by other evidence to be substantial grounds for impeachment of the President.

In refusing to produce these papers and things, Richard M. Nixon, substituting his judgment as to what materials were necessary for the inquiry, interposed the powers of the Presidency against the lawful subpoenas of the House of Representatives, thereby assuming for himself functions and judgments necessary to the exercise of the sole power of impeachment vested by the Constitution in the House of Representatives.

In all this, Richard M. Nixon has acted in a manner contrary to his trust as President and subversive of constitutional government, to the great prejudice of the cause of law and justice, and to the manifest injury of the people of the United States.

Wherefore, Richard M. Nixon, by such conduct, warrants impeachment and trial and removal from office.

This version from *The End of a Presidency*, the staff of the *New York Times*, New York: Holt, Rinehart and Winston, 1974.

Document 13: Nixon Announces His Resignation

Nixon realized that he had lost his support in the government by August 8, 1974. By then, the "smoking gun" conversation of June 23, 1972 had been made public and the House Judiciary Committee had approved three articles of impeachment against him. Knowing he would not survive the impeachment hearings, and understanding that he could no longer govern effectively, Nixon announced in a televised address that he would resign from office the next day, August 9, 1974.

Good evening.

This is the 37th time I have spoken to you from this office in which so many decisions have been made that shape the history of this nation.

Each time I have done so to discuss with you some matters that I believe affected the national interest. And all the decisions I have made in my public life I have always tried to do what was best for the nation.

Throughout the long and difficult period of Watergate, I have felt it was my duty to persevere; to make every possible effort to complete the term of office to which you elected me.

In the past few days, however, it has become evident to me that I no longer have a strong enough political base in the Congress to justify continuing that effort.

As long as there was such a base, I felt strongly that it was necessary to see the constitutional process through to its conclusion; that to do otherwise would be unfaithful to the spirit of that deliberately difficult process, and a dangerously destabilizing precedent for the future. But with the disappearance of that base, I now believe that the constitutional purpose has been served. And there is no longer a need for the process to be prolonged.

I would have preferred to carry through to the finish whatever the personal agony it would have involved, and my family unanimously urged me to do so.

But the interests of the nation must always come before any personal considerations. From the discussions I have had with Congressional and other leaders I have concluded that because of the Watergate matter I might not have the support of the Congress that I would consider necessary to back the very difficult decisions and carry out the duties of this office in the way the interests of the nation will require.

I have never been a quitter. To leave office before my term is completed is opposed to every instinct in my body. But as president I must put the interests of America first.

America needs a full-time president and a full-time Congress, particularly at this time with problems we face at home and abroad.

To continue to fight through the months ahead for my personal vindication would almost totally absorb the time and attention of both the president and the Congress in a period when our entire focus should be on the great issues of peace abroad and prosperity without inflation at home.

Therefore, I shall resign the presidency effective at noon tomorrow. Vice President Ford will be sworn in as president at that hour in this office.

Richard Nixon, resignation announcement, August 8, 1974.

CHRONOLOGY

JANUARY 9, 1913
Richard M. Nixon is born to Frank and Hannah Nixon in Yorba Linda, California.

JUNE 1937
Nixon graduates third in his class from Duke University Law School.

JUNE 21, 1940
Nixon marries Patricia Ryan.

JUNE 1943–JULY 1944
Nixon serves as a naval officer in the Pacific during World War II.

FEBRUARY 1946
The Nixons' first daughter, Patricia, is born.

NOVEMBER 1946
Nixon is elected to the House of Representatives as a Republican from California.

JULY 1947
Nixon travels to Europe as a member of a House committee investigating aid to European countries.

JUNE–AUGUST 1948
As a member of the House Committee on Un-American Activities, Nixon gains national fame by proving alleged communist sympathizer Alger Hiss guilty of perjury.

JULY 1948
The Nixons' second daughter, Julie, is born.

NOVEMBER 1950
Nixon is elected to the Senate from California, and is considered

as a possible vice presidential candidate for 1952.

SEPTEMBER 23, 1952
Nixon makes his famous Checkers speech on national television, in which he denies all claims of financial impropriety and plays for the sympathy of the American public by referring to "Checkers," his family's dog. Resounding public support allows Nixon to remain on the Republican Party's presidential ticket.

NOVEMBER 1952
Republican Dwight D. Eisenhower and running mate Richard M. Nixon win the presidential election.

NOVEMBER 1956
Eisenhower and Nixon are re-elected.

1958–1959
Nixon expands his foreign policy credentials with visits to South America and the Soviet Union.

NOVEMBER 1960
Nixon loses the presidential election to democratic candidate John F. Kennedy. Kennedy expands American involvement in the Vietnam War.

NOVEMBER 1962
Nixon loses the California gubernatorial election to democratic incumbent Edmund G. "Pat" Brown.

1964–1965
As a private citizen, Nixon makes visits to South Vietnam.

MARCH 31, 1968
Kennedy's successor, Lyndon B. Johnson, announces he will not seek re-election in 1968. A second democratic contender, Robert F. Kennedy, is assassinated on June 5.

NOVEMBER 1968
Richard Nixon is elected president of the United States over democratic candidate Hubert Humphrey. He is inaugurated on January 20, 1969.

MARCH 16, 1969
Nixon approves the secret bombing of Cambodia.

NOVEMBER 3, 1969
Citing the support of the "silent majority" of Americans, Nixon announces a plan to pursue a negotiated peace, combined with American troop withdrawals, in Vietnam.

JANUARY 1970
In his State of the Union address, Nixon makes a call for action on the environment.

MARCH 18, 1970
Prince Sihanouk of Cambodia is overthrown by General Lon Nol. Nixon chooses to use American force to aid the subsequent South Vietnamese invasion of Cambodia. This expansion of the Vietnam conflict inspires large antiwar protests in the United States.

MAY 4, 1970
Four students are killed during antiwar protests at Kent State University.

DECEMBER 2, 1970
The Environmental Protection Agency is opened.

FEBRUARY 1971
American forces support a South Vietnamese incursion into Laos.

MAY 20, 1971
Nixon announces significant progress on Strategic Arms Limitation Talks (SALT) with the Soviet Union.

JUNE 13, 1971
The *New York Times* begins to publish the Pentagon Papers. Their source, Daniel Ellsberg, becomes a target of Nixon's Plumbers, a White House unit created to plug information leaks.

SEPTEMBER 4, 1971
Ellsberg's psychiatrist's office is burglarized by Plumbers E. Howard Hunt and G. Gordon Liddy.

JANUARY 13, 1972

Nixon announces the withdrawal of 70,000 more American troops from Vietnam.

FEBRUARY 1972

Nixon's visit to China begins an era of open relations between the two countries.

MARCH 30, 1972

The Watergate break-in is allegedly approved by John Mitchell, attorney general and director of the Committee to Re-elect the President.

APRIL 16, 1972

In response to its invasion of South Vietnam, Nixon approves heavy bombing of North Vietnam.

MAY 20, 1972

Nixon's first summit meeting with Soviet leaders takes place in Moscow.

JUNE 17, 1972

Members of the Plumbers are arrested in the Democratic National Headquarters in the Watergate building in Washington, D.C.

JUNE 23, 1972

Nixon approves a plan to cover-up the Watergate break-in by interfering with the FBI investigation. The conversation is taped.

SEPTEMBER 15, 1972

Federal judge John Sirica indicts the Watergate burglars.

OCTOBER 1972

National Security Adviser Henry Kissinger resumes cease-fire negotiations with North Vietnam.

NOVEMBER 1972

Nixon is re-elected president by a huge margin.

DECEMBER 1972
Nixon approves the "Christmas Bombing" against North Vietnam in order to force them to return to negotiations. The bombing is the largest in U.S. history.

JANUARY 27, 1973
Nixon announces a cease-fire in Vietnam, thus ending American involvement in the conflict.

FEBRUARY 7, 1973
The Senate begins its Watergate investigation.

MARCH 13, 1973
Nixon, his chief of staff H.R. Haldeman, and special counsel John Dean meet, and allegedly discuss payoffs to silence the Watergate burglars.

MARCH 21, 1973
Nixon and Dean discuss further payoffs. Haldeman, Dean, and domestic adviser John Ehrlichman discuss the possibility of testimony with Nixon.

APRIL 30, 1973
Nixon announces the resignations of Haldeman, Ehrlichman, and Dean.

JUNE 25–29, 1973
Dean implicates Nixon in the cover-up of Watergate in nationally televised testimony before the Senate Watergate committee.

JULY 16, 1973
White House aide Alexander Butterfield announces the existence of Nixon's secret taping system. Nixon refuses to turn over the tapes relevant to the Watergate investigation.

OCTOBER 10, 1973
Vice President Spiro Agnew resigns in the face of tax evasion and other charges.

OCTOBER 20, 1973

In the "Saturday night massacre," Nixon orders the firing of Watergate special prosecutor Archibald Cox. In response, Attorney General Elliot Richardson quits and Deputy Attorney General William Ruckelshaus is fired.

OCTOBER 30, 1973

The House of Representatives begins examining articles of impeachment against Nixon.

FEBRUARY 1974

Sirica's grand jury names Nixon an unindicted co-conspirator in the Watergate cover-up.

FEBRUARY 25, 1974

In a nationally televised speech, Nixon pledges never to resign from office.

JULY 24, 1974

The Supreme Court rules that Nixon must turn over the White House tapes requested by new special prosecutor Leon Jaworski.

JULY 30, 1974

The House of Representatives approves three articles of impeachment against Nixon. They include accusations of obstruction of justice, abuse of power, and interfering with congressional investigations.

AUGUST 5, 1974

Nixon admits that he was involved in the Watergate cover-up as early as June 1972.

AUGUST 9, 1974

Nixon resigns as president, effective at noon. He is succeeded by Gerald Ford.

APRIL 22, 1994

Nixon dies.

FOR FURTHER RESEARCH

GENERAL

STEPHEN E. AMBROSE, *Nixon, Vol. I: The Education of a Politician 1913–1962*. New York: Simon and Schuster, 1987.

STEPHEN E. AMBROSE, *Nixon, Vol. II: The Triumph of a Politician 1962–1972*. New York: Simon and Schuster, 1989.

MONICA CROWLEY, *Nixon in Winter: His Final Revelations About Diplomacy, Watergate, and Life out of the Arena*. New York: Simon and Schuster, 1998.

JOHN EHRLICHMAN, *Witness to Power: The Nixon Years*. New York: Simon and Schuster, 1982.

LEON FRIEDMAN AND WILLIAM F. LEVANTROSSER, eds., *Richard M. Nixon: Politician, President, Administrator*. Westport, CT: Greenwood Press, 1991. Prepared under the auspices of Hofstra University.

LEONARD GARMENT, *Crazy Rhythm: My Journey from Brooklyn, Jazz and Wall Street to Nixon's White House, Watergate and Beyond*. New York: Times Books, 1997.

KENNETH FRANKLIN KURZ, *Nixon's Enemies*. Los Angeles: Lowell House, 1998.

RICHARD M. NIXON, *In the Arena*. New York: Simon and Schuster, 1990.

———, *RN, The Memoirs of Richard Nixon*. New York: Grosset and Dunlap, 1978.

HERBERT S. PARMET, *Richard Nixon and His America*. Boston: Little, Brown, 1990.

WILLIAM SAFIRE, *Before the Fall: An Inside View of the Pre-Watergate White House*. New York: Doubleday, 1975.

JOSEPH C. SPEAR, *Presidents and the Press: The Nixon Legacy*. Cambridge, MA: MIT Press, 1984.

TOM WICKER, *The Nixon Years 1969–1974: White House to Watergate.* New York: Abbeville, 1999.

FOREIGN POLICY

WILLIAM BURR, ed., *The Kissinger Transcripts.* New York: New Press, 1998.

LEON FRIEDMAN AND WILLIAM F. LEVANTROSSER, eds., *Richard M. Nixon: Cold War Patriot and Statesman.* Westport, CT: Greenwood Press, 1993. Prepared under the auspices of Hofstra University.

P. EDWARD HALEY, *Congress and the Fall of South Vietnam and Cambodia.* Rutherford, NJ: Fairleigh Dickinson University Press, 1982.

ARNOLD R. ISAACS, *Pawns of War: Cambodia and Laos.* Boston: Boston Publishing Co., 1987.

HENRY KISSINGER, *The White House Years.* Boston: Little, Brown, 1979.

RICHARD M. NIXON, *No More Vietnams.* New York: Arbor House, 1985.

TAD SZULC, *The Illusion of Peace: Foreign Policy in the Nixon Years.* New York: Viking Press, 1978.

WATERGATE

CARL BERNSTEIN AND BOB WOODWARD, *All the President's Men.* New York: Simon and Schuster, 1974.

LEN COLODNY AND ROBERT GETTLIN, *Silent Coup: The Removal of a President.* New York: St. Martin's Press, 1991.

FRED EMERY, *Watergate: The Corruption of American Politics and the Fall of Richard Nixon.* New York: Times Books, 1994.

SAM J. ERVIN, JR., *The Whole Truth: The Watergate Conspiracy.* New York: Random House, 1980.

LEON FREIDMAN AND WILLIAM F. LEVANTROSSER, eds., *Watergate and Afterward: The Legacy of Richard Nixon.* Westport, CT: Greenwood Press, 1992. Prepared Under the auspices of Hofstra University.

STANLEY I. KUTLER, *The Wars of Watergate: The Last Crisis of Richard Nixon*. New York: W.W. Norton, 1992.

STANLEY I. KUTLER, ed., *Abuse of Power: The New Nixon Tapes*. New York: Touchstone Books, 1998.

THE STAFF OF THE *NEW YORK TIMES*, *The End of a Presidency*. New York: Holt, Rinehart and Winston, 1973, 1974.

RONALD E. PYNN, *Watergate and the American Political Process*. New York: Praeger, 1975.

THEODORE H. WHITE, *Breach of Faith: The Fall of Richard Nixon*. New York: Atheneum Publishers, 1975.

BOB WOODWARD, *Shadow: Five Presidents and the Legacy of Watergate 1974–1999*. New York: Simon and Schuster, 1999.

INDEX

Abplanalp, Bob, 185–86
Abrams, Creighton, 84–85, 86
African Americans, 21–23
Agnew, Spiro, 41
Agreement on Ending the War and
  Restoring Peace in Vietnam, 121
air pollution
  cleaning up, from federal facilities,
    60
  efforts to reduce, 57–58
  legislation on, 49–50
  Nixon on, 72, 74
Aitken, Jonathan, 183
Albert, Carl, 201
Ambrose, Stephen, 185–86
American Civil Liberties Union
  (ACLU), 105
antiwar movement
  and Cambodia bombings, 101,
    102–105
  and Cambodia invasion, 32, 109,
    111
  and ending the draft, 80–81,
    112–13
  and military casualty rate, 111–12
  Nixon's response to, 105–106, 110
  and North Vietnam bombings, 34
  sought out by Nixon, 108–109
Arends, Leslie, 91
arms race, 25, 28
automotive emissions, 57–58, 68,
  76–77

Ball, George W., 145
Beecher, Bill, 90
Beisner, Robert, 103–104
Brown, Sam, 113
Brown v. Board of Education, 21, 22
Buchanan, Patrick J., 118

Bull, Stephen, 197
busing, 21–22
Butler, Caldwell, 195
Butterfield, Alexander, 158

Cambodia bombing/invasion, 26,
  32–33, 100–102
  backing off of, 105–106
  vs. bombing in North Vietnam,
    85–87
  covering up, 88–91
  failure of, 91–92
  under Johnson administration,
    82–84
  Nixon administration on, 84–85
  protests against, 32, 109, 102–105,
    111
  secrecy of, 87–88
  and Vietnamization, 31
Camilleri, Joseph, 136
Canada, 146
Carson, Rachel, 20, 64, 70
Caulfield, Jack, 187
Chambers, Whitaker, 14
Chatfield, Charles, 99
Checkers speech, 14–16
Chiang Kai-shek, 25
China
  Cultural Revolution in, 28–29
  and Vietnam policy, 82
  see also Chinese-American
    relations, normalizing
Chinese-American relations,
  normalizing, 28–30
  boldness of leaders in, 130
  China's dominant role in Asia
    through, 143, 144
  Chinese motives, 145–46
  Chinese opposition to, 135

international reactions to, 143–44
limiting Nixon's visit to China,
140–41
as more important than anti-
Communism, 133–34
Nixon's risk in, 134–35
and Nixon's visit to China,
125–26, 127
as public relations move, 150–52
as secretive, 148–50
and renouncing power ambitions,
141–42
and Soviet Union, 126, 131–32
and Taiwan issue, 127–28, 142–43
timing of, 146–48
U.S. motivation for, 134
and U.S. role in Asia, 126–27
and U.S. troop withdrawal from
Asia, 132
Vietnam experience influencing,
137–40
Chou En-lai, 146
Christmas bombings, 34, 121
CIA (Central Intelligence Agency),
157
civil rights, 21–23
Clean Air Act, 21, 51
amendments weakening, 50, 52
Clean Waters Restoration Act
(1966), 58
Clifford, Clark M., 83–84
Colodny, Len, 184
Colson, Charles, 37, 167, 186
Committee to Re-elect the
President, 117
Commoner, Barry, 63–64, 72, 73–74
communism
and Chinese-American relations,
vs. opposition to, 133–34
and Cold War, 24–25
saving South Vietnam from, 94–96
Concerned Officers Movement, 105
Congress
blamed for Vietnam policy, 122
and Cambodia bombings, 91

relationship with Nixon, 19
Consolidated Edison, 70
containment policy, 24–25, 143
Corps of Civil Engineers, 57
Counsel to the Committee to Re-
elect the President (CRP), 189
Cox, Archibald, 40, 158–59, 165
Crabb, Cecil V., 124
Cultural Revolution, 28–29

Davis, Glenn, 202
Dean, John, 167
allegations against Nixon, 170–71
on his role in Watergate, 190
implicating Nixon, 39–40, 157–58,
170–71
interest in DNC headquarters,
187–89
Watergate break-in commanded
by, 189–92
DeBenedetti, Charles, 99
Democratic National Convention
(1968), 18
Democratic National Headquarters
(DNC), 37, 187–89, 191
see also Watergate break-in
demonstrations. See antiwar
movement
détente, 27–28
DiMona, Joseph, 169
Dirksen, Everett, 91
draft, ending, 80–81, 112–13
DuBridge, Lee, 55, 58
Duke University Law School, 13
Dumelle, Jacob, 67

Earth Day (1970), 20, 71
Economic Club of Detroit, 74
Ehrlichman, John, 20
and environmental issues, 20, 75,
76, 77
and Watergate break-in, 171, 172
Eisenhower, Dwight D., 14, 16, 181
Eisenhower, Julie, 200
elections. See presidential elections

Ellsberg, Daniel, 36–37, 156, 177–78
Environmental Defense Fund, 70
environmental impact statement, 48
environmental issues, 20–21
  achievements made on, 46–50
  and America's high standard of
    living, 64–65
  business as priority over, 73–75
  and national park system, 60–61
  Nixon administration's foresight
    on, 61–62
  Nixon's centrist position on, 76–77
  Nixon's interest in, 54–55
    con, 75–76
    as questionable, 50–52
  Nixon's legacy on, 52–53
  Nixon vs. Congress on, 66–68
  prioritizing business over, 65–66,
    73–75
  public interest in, 63–64
  public opinion influencing
    decisions on, 68–71, 73, 76
  reducing pollution, 57–60
Environmental Protection Agency
  (EPA)
  and Armco Steel case, 51
  creation of, 46–47, 56–57
  OMB authority over, 73
  weakening regulations of, 51–52
Environmental Quality Council, 55
EPA. See Environmental Protection
  Agency (EPA)
Ervin, Sam, 39, 165
executive privilege, 158–59

Federal Water Pollution Control Act
  (1972), 50
Finch, Robert H., 56, 58
Flanigan, Peter, 51
Ford, Gerald, 43, 91
foreign policy. See Chinese-
  American relations, normalizing;
  Vietnam War
France, 140
Freedom Deal (code name), 90

Garfinkle, Adam, 107
Garment, Leonard, 200
Genovese, Michael A., 114
Gettlin, Robert, 184
Goheen, Robert, 103
Goldwater, Barry, 70
Good Luck (code name), 90–91
Gray, Patrick, 38, 165
Green, Marshall, 143, 144
Greenspan, Alan, 197, 200

Haig, Alexander, 88, 89, 91, 161–62,
  197, 200
Haldeman, Bob, 19
  and Lawrence O'Brien story,
    186–87
  and Vietnam conflict, 89, 91,
    115–16
  and Watergate, 38, 165, 167, 169,
    171, 185–86
Hamby, Alonzo L., 164
Hardin, Clifford M., 56
Hersh, Seymour, 89
Hesburgh, Theodore, 103
Hickel, Walter J., 56, 66
Hiss, Alger, 13–14
Ho Chi Minh, 26
Ho Chi Minh Trail, 32–33
Hoff, Joan, 79
House Committee on Un-American
  Activities, 14
HUD (Housing and Urban
  Development), 66
Hughes, Howard, 186–87
Humphrey, Hubert H., 18, 71
Hunt, E. Howard, 37, 38, 164–65,
  171, 188, 189, 192
hydro-electric power, 65–66

impeachment
  of Andrew Johnson, 160
  calls for Nixon's, 41, 43, 160–61
  vs. resignation, 193–96
India, 148–49
Internal Revenue Service (IRS), 156

Jackson, Henry, 48
Jackson State University, 32, 109
Japan, 127
Jaworski, Leon, 41, 166
Johnson, Andrew, 160
Johnson, Lyndon, 181
  Cambodia bombing under, 82–83
  on the environment, 70–71
  power exerted by, 162
  and Vietnam War, 26, 95, 97

Kennedy, John F., 181
  as Nixon's opponent, 16, 17
  and Vietnam War, 26, 95
Kent State University shootings, 32,
  103, 109
Khan, Sultan Mohammed, 149
Kilpatrick, James, 194, 196
Kimball, Jeffrey P., 118, 119
Kissinger, Henry, 19
  and antiwar movement, 103, 105
  and Cambodia bombing, 89, 91
  and China, 125, 130, 140, 150
  on environmentalism, 71
  negotiations with
    North Vietnam, 33, 34, 81, 116,
      117
    South Vietnam, 120
  on North Vietnamese
    communism, 94
Kleindeinst, Richard, 165
Krogh, Egil, 37, 55
Krushchev, Nikita, 16
Kutler, Stanley I., 193

Laird, Melvin, 19, 91
  and Cambodia invasion, 84, 85–86
  and U.S. troop reduction, 97
Land and Water Conservation
  Fund, 61
Landgrebe, Earl, 196
Laos, 26, 32–33, 80, 90–91, 115
Le Duc Tho, 33, 115, 116, 120
legislation, environmental, 47–50,
  58, 71

Liddy, Gordon, 37, 38, 178, 188, 189,
  191, 192
Lindsay, John, 72
Lin Piao, 135
Lon Nol (Prince), 32–33, 100
lottery system, 112

McClory, Robert, 201
McCord, James, 38, 39, 156–57
McGovern, George, 39, 166–67
Magruder, Jeb, 37, 39, 178, 188, 189,
  190–91, 192
Mahon, George H., 91
Manac'h, Etienne M., 147
Mao Tse-tung, 25, 130, 146, 148
Menu (code name), 87–88, 90
  see also Cambodia bombing/
    invasion
military
  casualties, 30, 81, 111
  ending draft for, 112–13
  number sent to Vietnam, 26–27
  withdrawal from Asia, 132
  see also Vietnamization
Mitchell, John, 19, 37, 167, 188,
  189–90
Moore, Richard, 197
Muskie, Edmund, 48, 64, 66

National Environmental Policy Act
  (1969), 48, 66
National Park System, 60–61
National Petition Committee, 105
National Resources Defense
  Council, 73
Neal, Arthur G., 154
Nguyen Van Thieu, 81, 84, 120, 121
Nixon, Donald, 186
Nixon, Frank (father), 12
Nixon, Hannah (mother), 12
Nixon, Julie (daughter), 13
Nixon, Patricia, 13
Nixon, Richard M.
  and Alger Hiss case, 13–14
  on antiwar movement, 32,

105–106, 108–109, 110
approval rating of, 111
birth of, 12
calls for impeachment of, 41, 43,
    160–61
Checkers speech by, 14–15
on civil rights issues, 21–23
Cold War, influence of, 24–25
as a criminal, 154
departure from White House,
    204–205
education, 12–13
election losses, 16–17
enemies of, 168, 170
as expert in foreign policy,
    107–108
insecurities of, 173–75
last day as president, 202
and Lawrence O'Brien story,
    186–87
in 1968 election, 17–18
presidency of, approach to, 18–20
presidential legacy of, 12
resignation of, 42–43, 162,
    200–202
on resignation vs. impeachment,
    193–96
    speech on, 202–204
Soviet Union policy, 27–28
use of "executive privilege,"
    158–59
use of personal power, 162–63
as vice-president, 15–16
as villain, questioning, 184
as well trained for presidency,
    176–77
withdrawal of U.S. troops by, 111
see also Chinese-American
    relations, normalizing;
    environmental issues; Vietnam
    War; Watergate break-in
Nixon Doctrine, 132–33
No More Vietnams (Nixon), 80
North Vietnam, 26
    and Cambodia, 32, 80, 82

negotiations with, 33, 34–35, 81,
    82, 116, 117, 120
U.S. bombing of, 33–34, 116–17,
    121

O'Brien, Lawrence, 186–87, 192
Office of Management and Budget
    (OMB), 21, 51–52, 73
Office of Minority Business
    Enterprise (OMBE), 22
OMB. See Office of Management
    and Budget (OMB)
Operation Gemstone, 187–91

Pakistan, 140, 148–49
Palmer, William W., 92
Paris Peace Accords, 34–35
Patio (code name), 89–90
Peale, Norman Vincent, 195
Pentagon Papers, 36, 156, 177–78
People's Republic of China, 82
    see also China
Petersen, Henry, 172
Podhoretz, Norman, 93
pollution. See air pollution; water
    pollution
presidential elections
    1952, 14–15
    1960, 16
    1968, 17–18
Price, Ray, 116
prostitution ring, 188–89, 191
protests. See antiwar movement
public schools, 21–22

Rebozo, Bebe, 185, 186
"Report on Selected Air and
    Ground Operations in Cambodia
    and Laos" (U.S. Department of
    Defense), 91
Reschauer, Edwin, 103
Richardson, Elliot, 40, 91, 159
Rivers, Mendel, 91
Roosevelt, Theodore, 70
Royko, Mike, 112–13

Ruckelshaus, William D., 40, 47, 51–52, 159
Russell, Richard, 91
Ryan, Patricia. *See* Patricia Nixon

Safire, William, 49
SALT I (Strategic Arms Limitation Treaty), 28
"Saturday night massacre," 40–41, 159
Saxbe, William, 194
Schell, Jonathan, 198–99
Schelling, Thomas, 103
Schlesinger, James, 91, 161
school integration, 21–22
Sheehan, Neil, 96
Sierra Club, 64
Silent Coup (Coldney and Gettlin), 184, 188, 189
Silent Spring (Carson), 20, 64, 70
Silver, Rabbi Samuel, 195–96
Sino-American relations. *See* Chinese-American relations, normalizing
Sirica, John J., 38, 39, 156
Sitton, Ray B., 88, 89, 91, 92
Snow, Edgar, 148
South Vietnam, 26
    Cambodia invasion by, 32, 100
    Laos invasion by, 32–33, 115
    saving from communism, 94–96
    U.S. negotiating away, 117, 120
Soviet Union, 27–28
    and arms race, 25
    and Chinese-American relations, 126
    and military power in Asia, 127
    and Vietnam policy, 82
Stans, Maurice H., 18, 22, 176
Stennis, John C., 91
Storm King Mountain, 70
supersonic air transport plane, 67–68
Sutter, Robert G., 129

Taipei, 144
Taiwan, 25, 127–28, 142–43, 144
Thompson, Sir Robert, 95–96
Train, Russell E., 47, 51–52
Truman, Harry, 163, 181

Ulasewicz, Tony, 187–88
U.S. Congress. *See* Congress; legislation
U.S. Department of Environment and Natural Resources, 57
U.S. Department of Natural Resources and the Environment, 46–47
U.S. Forest Service, 57
U.S. Supreme Court, 159

Vann, John Paul, 96
Vietnamization, 31, 84–85, 95–98
    and Cambodia invasion, 101–102
    and Chinese-American relations, 139
Vietnam War, 25–27, 30–35
    and Chinese-American relations, 137–40
    and Laos invasion, 32–33
    and negotiations, 33, 34, 116, 117, 120
    Nixon
        depicted as peacemaker in, 118–19
        effort of, to end, 115–16
        failure in, 122
        view of/intentions on, 80–82, 93–94, 115–16
    peace agreement in, 34–35, 121–22
    as saving South Vietnam from communism, 94–95
    U.S. aggression on North Vietnam, 32–33, 116–17, 121
    U.S. air power in, 33–34
    U.S. role in Asia following, 126
    see also antiwar movement; Cambodia bombing/invasion; Vietnamization

Volpe, John A., 56, 58
Voorhis, Jerry, 13, 63

Warren, Charles S., 45
Warren, Earl, 105
Watergate break-in, 108–109
  and abuses of power, 160, 162–63
  and allegations against Nixon,
    157–58, 170–71
  background to, 35–36, 177–78
  beginning of, 155
  and bugging Lawrence O'Brien,
    186–87
  and call for Nixon's impeachment,
    41, 43, 160–61
  commanded by John Dean,
    187–92
  coverup for, 38–40, 156–57
  Nixon's reasons for, 178–80
  impeachment vs. resignation for,
    193–96
  and Nixon's enemies, 155–56, 168,
    170
  Nixon's first reaction to, 185–86
  and Nixon's insecurities, 173–75
  Nixon's lack of knowledge on, 185,
    188
  and Nixon's mean-spiritedness,
    166–68
  Nixon's opportunities to survive,
    171–72
  and Nixon's resignation, 161–62

people involved, 36–38, 164–65
public response to, 198–99
questioning history's version of,
  184–85
Republic staff response to, 196–97,
  200
summary of, 165–66
support for Nixon on, 196
timing of, 181–82
as unnecessary, 169
and White House tapes, 40–42,
  158–60, 170, 172–73, 180–81
water pollution
  cleaning up federal facilities from,
    60
  efforts to reduce, 58–59
  expenditures cut for, 67
  legislation on, 49, 50
Water Quality Improvement Act
  (1969), 66
Wells, Maxie, 192
Whitaker, John C., 54, 70, 73
"White Paper," 88, 90, 91
Whittier College, 13
Wicker, Tom, 69

Yahya Khan, 148
Yale University, 102–103

Zhou Enlai, 130, 133, 135, 140
Ziegler, Ron, 37